Brittle Stars
& Mudbugs

For the Rubida family,
Let's go back to
Hawaii !

Pator's

Brittle Stars & Mudbugs

An Uncommon
Field Guide

to Northwest Shorelines & Wetlands

Patricia K. Lichen

Illustrated by Linda M. Feltner

SASQUATCH BOOKS
SEATTLE

Printed in Canada
Distributed in Canada by Raincoast Books, Ltd.
07 06 05 04 03 02 01   6 5 4 3 2 1

Cover and interior design and composition: Kate Basart
Copy editor: Alice Copp Smith

Library of Congress Cataloging in Publication Data
Brittle stars and mudbugs : an uncommon field guide to Northwest shorelines and wetlands / by Patricia Lichen ; illustrations by Linda Feltner.
        p.   cm.
        refereneces; index.
        1. Natural history—Northwest, Pacific. 2. Coastal animals—Northwest, Pacific—Identification. 3. Coastal plants—Northwest, Pacific—Identification. 4. Wetland animals—Northwest, Pacific—Identification. 5. Wetland plants—Northwest, Pacific—Identification. I. Title
QH104.5.N6L528 2001
508.795—dc21   00-052260

Sasquatch Books
615 Second Avenue
Seattle, Washington 98104
(206) 467-4300
www.SasquatchBooks.com
books@SasquatchBooks.com

To my old Greenpeace buddies, now scattered to the four winds,
for the days when we worked to Save the Whales.

Contents

Acknowledgments

I am grateful to the following experts, each of whom graciously reviewed at least one (and more often several) of these essays: Ric Balfour of the Oregon Forest Resources Institute; John Calambokidis of the Cascadia Research Collective; Jim Cubbage; Teresa DeLorenzo of the Northwest Ecological Research Institute's Turtle Project; Esther Howard; Klaus Richter; Todd R. Seamons; Pete Taylor; and Brent Vadopalas. They pointed out errors and misinterpretations wherever these reared their ugly heads. Any inaccuracies that remain in these essays are mine alone.

The following people also supplied information for particular essays: Teresa DeLorenzo (Western Painted and Pond Turtles); Mike Kelly of the U.S. Fish and Wildlife Service and Jean McCrae of the Oregon Department of Fish & Wildlife (Signal Crayfish).

My thanks also to these friends and family members, who have shared with me encounters with the natural world and then allowed me to tell those stories: Daniel Burgevin; my sister-in-law Anne DeLano, and her brother, Tim Lichen; Diane Shew; Pete Taylor; Athel von Koettlitz; Jolyon Western; and Peter Willcox.

I am also indebted to my father, Frederick J. Hutchison, and the members of two writers' groups, Sirius Writers and Chrysalis, who critiqued and improved many of these essays. Special thanks to the stalwart Susan McElheran, who, in belonging to both groups, critiqued more of these essays than anyone short of my editor. Among the Sirius Writers, I especially thank Bonnie and Gale Long, Jim Manuel, Dwight Ball Morrill, Tawny Schlieski, and Cord "Bud" Sengstake. Among the Chrysalis group at Clackamas Community College, Oregon City, Oregon, I especially thank Beth Miles, who critiqued many essays outside of the meetings, and Kate Gray, our fearless leader. I am grateful to the members of both groups for their unfaltering encouragement and enthusiasm for this project.

Introduction

"The birds I heard today, which fortunately, did not come within the scope of my science, sang as freshly as if it had been the first morning of creation." I've always loved this quote by Henry David Thoreau, which reminds me that I don't need to know the name of a songbird (or a fern or a mushroom or a hawk, for that matter) to enjoy it.

Yet, as Thoreau certainly knew, there is joy in being able to recognize a plant or creature wherever we find it, and to greet it by name. As with our other friendships, the more we learn about a particular being's life, the greater our appreciation can grow.

This is the purpose of the *Uncommon Field Guide* series: to enhance our connection to other beings in the natural world, and hopefully to deepen that connection. Each of the three books (*Passionate Slugs & Hollywood Frogs: An Uncommon Field Guide to Northwest Backyards*; *Brittle Stars & Mudbugs: An Uncommon Field Guide to Northwest Shorelines & Wetlands*; and *River-Walking Songbirds & Singing Coyotes: An Uncommon Field Guide to Northwest Mountains*) offers an opportunity to become better acquainted with plants, animals, and phenomena (such as rainbows or lightning) found in the Pacific Northwest.

In each book I've focused on easily recognizable species and phenomena, and those common to a particular Pacific Northwest geographic area. Of course, some of the subjects do not neatly segregate themselves into specific territories, and for that reason their placement has been arbitrary. (For example, the American crow, coyote, and common horsetail might have ended up in any one of the three books—but the crows landed in the backyard book, coyote found a home in the mountain book, and horsetails sprouted in the shorelines and wetlands book.)

Similarly, some of the creatures within this *Northwest Shorelines & Wetlands* book refuse to confine themselves to either salt or fresh water.

For this reason, the essays segue from ocean and sandy beaches to rocky intertidal areas, blending into those species found in estuaries and leading, finally, to those whose habitat is fresh water.

With apologies to those of you living in the eastern part of Washington and Oregon, the essays in all three books focus to a greater degree on the region west of the Cascade Mountains. Please note I often use the shortcut of "Pacific Northwest region" instead of the more accurate (but too cumbersome) phrase "Pacific Northwest region west of the Cascades."

For many years I had the pleasure of working as a naturalist in Washington and Oregon, discussing with people the plants, animals, and natural events of the Northwest as we walked through woods and beside waterfalls, down into caves and along lakeshores. It's my hope that the *Uncommon Field Guide* series continues that work, acting in the capacity of a friendly naturalist who answers your questions, mentions interesting tidbits you might not think to ask, and helps to further both your understanding and your relationship with the natural world.

Harbor Seal

Latin name: *Phoca vitulina*

Description: 5 to 6 feet long; males slightly larger than females; mostly pale gray mottled with darker spots and rings, but may have extremely pale markings or may be dark overall.

Habitat: Harbors, beaches, mudflats, low rocks, and offshore waters.

I was sitting on the beach, watching my friend Jolyon surf, when a dog poked its head out of the water behind him. It took me a moment to realize that the "dog" was really a seal. Although I yelled and pointed, Jolyon couldn't hear me over the sound of the surf and never did turn around to see the ocean creature that trailed along behind him like a canine companion.

When harbor seals are in their element—water—they tend to be very curious. They check out boaters as well as surfers, and will swim parallel to people walking along the shoreline. But when they "haul out" onto land, seals are wary and vulnerable. Even when lounging like overinflated sausages, they are aware when people come uncomfortably close. If they feel threatened, they hump across the beach to reach the safety of the sea. (Seals can't rotate their back flippers underneath themselves to walk on them as do sea lions.)

But underwater, it's people who are ungainly and awkward in comparison. Harbor seals glide and gambol, using their powerful hind flippers as propulsion and adjusting course with a flick of their front flippers. As the animal dives, it closes off nostrils and earholes, and its heart rate slows down to one-tenth of its capacity. Blood flow remains strong to the brain and heart but dawdles to the extremities. A harbor seal can hold its breath for twenty minutes in dives that reach nearly three hundred feet below the surface. But most of the time the seal is underwater for just three to five minutes before popping its head above the surface for a quick, inquiring look around.

During its dives, a seal might be foraging for crabs, squid, octopus, or fish. Harbor seals, unlike their larger salmon-loving cousins, the sea lions, seem content to feed mostly on noncommercial fish like eelpout and rockfish. But before this was general knowledge, and before the passage of the Marine Mammal Protection Act, fishermen and state authorities attempted to eradicate harbor seals from Northwest waters. An estimated seventeen thousand animals were killed between 1947 and 1960. Today the harbor seal's chief predator is not people but its ancient nemesis, the killer whale.

Despite their ease in the water, seals must come ashore to mate and give birth. Unlike many of their pinniped relations (sea lions, seals, and walruses), harbor seals don't form large breeding colonies overseen by a single male. Instead, both sexes couple promiscuously with whoever strikes their fancy. Pups are born between April and July. When the babies are very young, they are unable to keep up with their foraging mothers. This isn't usually a problem; the mother simply leaves her baby on a convenient beach while she feeds, afterward returning to collect her child. The glitch in the harbor seals' daycare system is that well-meaning, uninformed people "rescue" the pups, delivering them to police officers, vets, or other inappropriate foster mothers.

So, if you should you find a pup on the beach, let it be. If you are concerned that its mother has been gone overly long (keep in mind that she may leave the pup for more than twenty-four hours), contact the state's department of fish and wildlife, a local animal shelter, or a marine mammal stranding network. *Never* take a pup off the beach yourself, despite its adorable looks and its big doelike eyes. Left alone, that baby will grow into an inquisitive adult who bobs up out of the water to watch people walking along the beach or surfing in the ocean.

Pacific White-Sided Dolphin

Latin name: *Lagenorhynchus obliquidens*

Description: To 7 or 8 feet long; snout blunt and short; black back; thin gray line streaks across flanks into large patch at rear; white shoulder and underside; sickle-shaped, two-toned dorsal fin, dark on leading edge, lighter on trailing edge.

Habitat: Along continental shelf, Northern Pacific Ocean, from Alaska to Baja California, Mexico; also occasionally in Puget Sound.

If asked to guess which cetacean (whale, dolphin, or porpoise) is most numerous in our coastal waters, many Northwesterners would name the gray whale, or perhaps the orca. But although they are seen by fewer people, Pacific white-sided dolphins greatly outnumber their larger cousins.

The people who do see these beautiful dolphins are fortunate, because these creatures can put on an exciting show. Especially acrobatic, they often leap high or even somersault out of the water, and they enjoy riding the bow waves of boats and playing in their wakes. Although they're often seen in small groups, a lucky boater might see schools numbering one thousand or more. They also chum around with other species, especially Risso's and Northern right whale dolphins.

These animals were once harassed and attacked by fishermen, who regarded them as competitors. Protected by law for decades now, white-sided dolphins are increasingly seen closer to shore and in inland waters. They are sometimes sighted during whale-watch tours or even from a shoreline promontory.

The dolphins eat small fish such as anchovies, hake, herring, and sardines, but their greatest prey is probably squid. They are quick, agile hunters who, like other toothed dolphins and whales, use echolocation to help find their meals. To do this, the dolphin emits a series of high-frequency clicks toward an object it wants to know more about. It produces these sounds in the nasal passages of its head and transmits them out in a narrow beam. When the sound beam hits an obstacle, echoes of the clicks bounce back to the dolphin, who then interprets them. The animal may sweep its head in an arc from side to side to get a more complete "view." From these sound pictures, the animal can recognize the distance to the object, its size, shape, and density, and even its texture.

Echolocation also enables dolphins to "see" inside each other's bodies and the bodies of other species. Captive dolphins of other species have shown interest in pregnant women in the water with them, repeatedly scanning their abdomens. One trainer I know received the first hint of her new pregnancy courtesy of the dolphin she worked with. These animals have also shown interest in bones that have been broken and other abnormalities.

Although Pacific white-sided dolphins have been successfully kept alive in oceanariums, relatively little is known about their habits in the wild. It is thought that they migrate slightly within their range, shifting north in the spring and south in the fall. Some researchers suggest that dolphins from Pacific Northwest waters may join a resident herd off Southern California in the winter months.

Mating occurs in the northern part of the range, in early summer or fall. The calves are born after about a year's gestation and are two and one-half to three feet in length. Like other cetacean young, they drink rich milk from either of two retractable nipples on the mother's underside.

The annual migration of gray whales through Pacific Northwest waters may draw more attention, and a family of majestic orcas might be more awe-inspiring, but in terms of sheer numbers, neither can match a thousand-strong gathering of Pacific white-sided dolphins. And should even a few dolphins start cavorting near a whale-watching boat, they might just steal the show.

Waves

Twenty-four hours a day, every day of the year, waves relentlessly march toward the shore to die. They are such an expected phenomenon that, even as you watch row after row stomping in and throwing themselves against the rocks or onto the beach, it might never occur to you to wonder where they come from.

Ocean winds generate these regimented waves, and the waves are unceasing because the winds are unceasing. Small waves will dissipate before ever meeting land, but larger waves brewed by storm winds can travel thousands of miles before reaching shore. The harder the winds blow and the longer the distance they blow over, the larger are the waves they generate. Because the Pacific Ocean is larger than the Atlantic, with wider stretches of open water, its waves are generally larger than those of the Atlantic.

Unless a wave is breaking, it doesn't actually move much water. Once you swim out past the breakers, an incoming swell will lift you up and down rather than bearing you directly back to the shore. This is because the motion within a swell on open water is more of a circular movement than a forward one. Although the wind begins to push the surface water forward, as the resulting swell gains height, gravity forces it back down. The water of the swell plunges below the surface, where it is shoved upward by water pressure—and so completes its circular route.

But a wave near shore encounters friction from the sea bottom. As the base of the wave drags against the sea bottom, the top of the wave continues to hurtle forward and begins to crest and break—it's almost as if the wave trips on the sea bottom in its rush toward shore. The wave breaks when the depth of the water it enters is about one and one-third times the height of the wave. A four-foot wave will break where the water is about five and a quarter feet deep. A large wave can break far offshore, creating smaller waves that break again as they near the shore. Noting where waves break can tell you the topography of the sea bottom just offshore. Waves consistently breaking at a particular spot offshore indicate a reef or some other raised area. An area lower than the surrounding seabed is revealed where waves are able to rush closer to shore before breaking.

The highest wave ever measured off the Northwest coast was ninety-five feet high, but circumstantial evidence suggests that the Pacific has delivered even higher waves here. During a winter storm that battered the Tillamook Rock lighthouse near the mouth of the Columbia River, a rock weighing more than a hundred pounds was hurtled through the roof of the lightkeeper's house, located one hundred feet above the water. The wave that threw the rock may have been one hundred and twelve feet high.

In addition to being created by ocean winds, huge waves can be generated by earthquakes or volcanic eruptions that shake the water and generate tsunamis ("soo-NAH-mees"), also known as "tidal waves" (a misnomer, since they are not associated with tides). A tsunami can pass unnoticed under a ship at sea yet rear up one hundred feet when it eventually reaches shallow water.

But the vast majority of the waves that reach the Pacific Northwest coastline are simple swells created by storms at sea. And they'll keep right on dashing themselves against our shores for as long as the winds do blow.

Gray Whale

Latin name: *Eschrichtius robustus*

Description: To 46 feet long, female slightly larger than male; mottled gray overall; 6 to 12 knobby "knuckles" (forming a dorsal hump) instead of dorsal fin.

Habitat: Grays travel south along the Pacific Coast from November to February but are closest to shore from February to June when traveling north (the earliest-leaving northbound whales will encounter the latest-arriving southbound whales). Peak migration in the Northwest occurs from mid-March to mid-April. Some animals remain in Northwest waters during the summer and do not migrate to the Bering Sea.

Peter, our captain, was fighting a losing battle. Every so often his voice squawked from the handheld radio, issuing increasingly terser demands that we return to the ship. But how could we? We'd found the gray whales—and they were mating.

Our ship, the *Rainbow Warrior,* was anchored in the waters off Baja California, and a group of us had piled into two inflatable boats and gone in search of the whales. Even though we were on a tight schedule and due to leave the area, the chance to see gray whales in their birthing and mating grounds was too good to pass up. As soon as someone spotted the first whale, we cut our outboard engines and drifted silently over the sparkling blue waves. Now Daniel grabbed the radio and crowed, "We'll be coming in right away, Capt'n—but there's three of them and we can see a red sea snake!" Not one of us moved to restart the engines.

The "sea snake" referred to a whale's penis, a surprisingly agile appendage. Usually tucked inside the streamlined male's body, the penis emerges from the genital slit during copulation or sex play. This tapering and supple member slides, taps, and rolls as it maneuvers across the broad expanse of the female's body, eventually seeking her genital slit. Mating gray whales often include a second male, who helps to support the female—or, it has been suggested, to prevent her from leaving. But we saw no hint of resistance in the slow rolls, sliding twists, and slippery undulations of these whales. When we voyeurs finally left, compelled by dire threats from the radio, the whales' tryst still continued in our wake.

We encountered the whales at the southern end of their annual migration. Grays divide their time between their winter breeding and birthing areas in Mexico and their summer feeding grounds in Arctic seas. In traveling the twelve thousand miles between the two places, they undertake the longest known migration of any mammal.

Their pattern of hugging the coast once made these whales especially vulnerable to whalers. In the mid-1800s they were mercilessly hunted until there were so few left it was no longer profitable to pursue them. Once they were left alone, their population rebounded, and in the early 1900s, the Pacific gray whale again became a target of whalers—this time with modern equipment. By 1946, when the whales received international protection, their population had again been decimated; it is estimated only a few thousand remained. Yet once again the population gradually rebuilt, and it is now believed to match or exceed pre-whaling numbers. By international agreement, only hunts by (or to benefit) Native peoples are currently allowed, though these are controversial.

Sadly, the Pacific gray whale's success has not been matched by other stocks. The Atlantic gray whale was hunted to extinction, and sightings of the Korean gray of the western Pacific are so rare that some experts consider it extinct.

That coast-hugging habit, which once drew whalers and now delights whale watchers, results from the animals' feeding style. Of all the great whale species, grays alone feed on the ocean bottom. Like most other whales, grays have baleen plates rather than teeth. Baleen, once called whalebone, is made of a horny material similar to our fingernails.

Hundreds of elongated triangular plates, packed close together, hang like vertical blinds from the upper jaw of the whale. The inside edges of the plates are fringed with coarse, thick bristles.

A gray whale feeds by lying against the sea bottom and sucking in shrimp and other small bottom-dwelling creatures, along with the sand or mud these are embedded in. The whale then uses its tongue to push water and sediment out of its mouth, through the narrow gaps between the baleen plates. The interior fringe of the baleen sieves the edible morsels, which the whale then swallows. Grays sometimes also take actual bites out of the ocean floor, leaving mouth-shaped pits behind. Most feeding grays settle against the sediment on their right sides (and have worn and abraded baleen on the right sides of their mouths), but a few are lefties.

Whether they are observed feeding, mating, or just spouting and swimming, it is a treat to see gray whales, and each sighting is made more precious by the knowledge that we nearly killed them all. One of my finest memories is of the day I sat with my *Rainbow Warrior* crewmates in drifting boats, watching the surging, sensuous whales, while Daniel kept promising our captain that we'd head back soon.

Orca

Latin name: *Orcinus orca*

Description: Females to 25 feet long, with dorsal fins to 3 feet tall; males to 30 feet, with dorsal fins to 6 feet tall; upper side black except for white patch behind eye and gray "saddle" just behind dorsal fin; underside white and black.

Habitat: Puget Sound, Strait of Juan de Fuca, around Vancouver Island, and northern coast of British Columbia; deep water.

The high, triangular dorsal fin and distinctive black and white coloration of the orca, or killer whale, may make it the most readily recognizable cetacean in the world. Despite that recognition, orcas have usually been seen as one-dimensional caricatures. From the earliest writings about them, by Pliny the Elder in the first century A.D., up until the last decades of the twentieth century, orcas were considered insatiable, bloodthirsty killers liable to attack anything in front of them—including people. Then, with their widespread introduction to marine parks in the late 1960s, the villains were transformed into frolicking clowns who waggishly stuck out their tongues and squirted audiences on command.

The true nature of these largest of dolphins is gradually being revealed through long-term research studies of wild orca populations in the Pacific Northwest. One of the most fascinating discoveries is the recognition of three separate groups of orcas that frequent the waters of British Columbia and Washington. The "residents," "transients," and "offshores" are distinct types of orcas, with subtle differences in the shape of their dorsal fins and saddle markings. Each also has its own vocalizations, feeding habits, and social structure—in short, different cultures. They do not interbreed or even intermingle. Although the ranges of the residents and transients overlap, they avoid each other.

The residents are the longest- and best-studied orca populations in the world. They are divided into northern and southern communities, with separate ranges. Most of the time these two large communities further divide themselves into smaller groupings. The basic social unit is a family composed of a mother and her descendants. It was initially assumed that males were "harem masters" who escorted their females and young. But any males in a group are actually the sons of a matriarch, who is also accompanied by her daughters and their offspring. These matriarchal groups may contain three or four generations.

In addition to staying in close physical proximity, the residents are a vocal lot. They communicate using a variety of whistles, shrieks, squawks, and squeals. Researchers can actually trace familial lineages by subtle differences in the "dialects" of different groups.

The transients, as the name implies, are more mobile than the residents, although they do at times share the same territory. One of the differences between residents and transients is their diet. Residents eat salmon and other fish. While in Northwest waters, transients apparently eat only warm-blooded prey: marine mammals like sea lions and seals, and the occasional sea bird (their year-round diet is not known). This group of orcas best fits the "killer whale" label; they do indeed attack and kill other whales, and in ways that seem merciless and cruel to human observers. Some unidentified orcas, suspected to be transients, have even been seen harassing and preying on deer that attempt to swim a narrow channel between two pieces of land.

Unlike the residents, the transient whales are relatively silent, probably to avoid alerting the prey to their presence. They are vociferous only during the attack and after it, but their repertoire of calls is not as extensive as that of the residents. No calls are common to both groups.

The transients' social structure is less stable than that of the residents: some adolescents may leave their mother's group, and bulls often travel alone. These shifting social groups may result from their choice of prey. Marine mammals are less abundant and less reliably present than fish, and their predators may adapt to social groupings that best fit their ability to feed.

The third orca group, the offshores, has been discovered relatively recently, and not much is known about them. Like the residents, they vocalize frequently and may eat only fish. Usually found in large groups of thirty to sixty individuals on the continental shelf, they seldom come into protected coastal waters.

Biologists estimate that orcas have been living in the waters of British Columbia and Washington for thousands of years. But today, researchers are increasingly concerned about the whales' future. Many young orcas have died in recent years, and their carcasses have revealed high levels of lead, mercury, and polychlorinated biphenyls (PCBs). Exposure to toxic substances is probably the greatest threat to this population, but researchers are also concerned about the decline in salmon populations (particularly chinook, which the residents strongly favor), and a variety of problems caused by increased boat traffic, including collisions, underwater noise pollution, and above-water exhaust pollution.

One researcher who has studied this whale population for over twenty years suggests that the next twenty-five years will determine whether orcas can continue to survive in Pacific Northwest waters.

Octopus

Latin names: *Octopus dofleini*; *O. rubescens*
Description: *O. dofleini*: arm length to 15 feet; usually gray or mottled brown; *O. rubescens*: arm length to 18 inches; usually red or mottled red and gray, both species can change color.
Habitat: Coastal or ocean waters, sometimes in rocky dens and crevices.

Our ship was dead in the water, floating on the vast Pacific, while the engineers tinkered down in the engine room. When Athel reached into the main sea suction box to clear it of debris, something grabbed his fingers. Snatching back his hand, he yelled, "It's got tentacles!" Indeed it had. The baby octopus he gingerly extracted a few minutes later had eight little tentacles, each just a couple of inches long.

I had spotted full-grown octopuses (not "octopi," according to those who study them) underwater before, crouched in rock crevices, but this soft baby was the first I'd ever touched. Peter, the captain of the *Rainbow Warrior*, and I donned snorkels, masks, and fins and went over the side of the ship to release the little mollusk. We played with it for a bit underwater, watching it swim and peeling its suckered arms off the ship when it grabbed hold. When the octopus had had enough of us, it loosed a tiny cloud of black ink and scooted away. Later I learned that the ink is not only a smoke screen, but also a stink bomb that stuns the olfactory abilities of pursuing predators.

Because my voyages on the *Rainbow Warrior* are long over, these days I hope to encounter another baby octopus in a tide pool. Two species are most likely to be found in Northwest tide pools or seen by divers. The giant

Pacific octopus (*Octopus dofleini*) and the red octopus (*O. rubescens*) can both be found in shallow water; the red octopus is more likely to be encountered. The giant Pacific octopus is the largest in the world; the record-setter weighed more than six hundred pounds and had an arm-spread of thirty-one feet. But the largest most divers can hope to see is closer to one hundred pounds, with a sixteen-foot armspread.

For many years the octopus was depicted as a fearsome monster liable to grab any passing ship and wrestle it down to the bottom of the ocean. In reality, octopuses are shy, spend a great deal of time hiding, and get into a wrestling match only with the crab they want for dinner.

Octopuses are now widely regarded as the most intelligent invertebrate (animal lacking a backbone). Scientists have taught them to run simple mazes, open jars and small doors, and distinguish shapes, colors, and textures. Captive octopuses recognize specific people (wild ones, too, sometimes become friendly with certain divers) and often endear themselves to their keepers. One clever octopus slithered out of its tank at night, ate fish in a nearby aquarium, and then returned to its own tank, thereby perplexing the scientist who, in the morning light, found an apparently undisturbed yet empty fish aquarium.

The octopus may need its more highly developed brain to coordinate all those arms, operate the thousands of suckers that both taste and touch, and control minuscule muscles that allow thousands of pigment sacs on its skin to change color to replicate its current background. An octopus makes a chameleon look boring by comparison; it can be any combination of red, brown, black, gray, yellow, or orange and can even change the texture of its skin.

Octopuses can flush red when they discover a member of the opposite sex, although the actual mating occurs without much fanfare. One of the male's tentacles has no suckers on its last six inches or so, and this arm is used to transfer a packet of sperm up under the mantle (the part that looks like a head) of the female. After she has laid her eggs in a protected place, the female tends them continuously for the next five or six months until they hatch. She usually takes no nourishment during this time, and dies shortly after the young struggle out of their eggs.

Whenever I peek into a tide pool, I hope to see a baby octopus. Who knows? I may have already looked at one without ever seeing it. Even very young octopuses are so adept at camouflage that, like our ship's engineer, I may have to be grabbed by its tentacles before noticing it.

Spiny Dogfish

Latin name: *Squalus acanthias*

Description: 3 to 4 feet long, rarely 5 feet; adults gray, sometimes brownish above and whitish below, juveniles have white spots; jutting spine just in front of each of two dorsal fins.

Habitat: From just offshore to 1,200 feet deep.

The spiny dogfish, by far the Pacific Northwest's most common shark, is more annoying than dangerous. Although dogfish may swim alongside divers and have an unnerving habit of sometimes veering abruptly toward them, they do not attack people. They eat fish, not the seals and sea lions that a larger shark might occasionally mistake a human for.

Dogfish are much more trouble to people who fish than to those who dive, surf, or swim. Because these sharks are attracted by the same bait that appeals to salmon, dogfish strike on fishing lines. And because they sometimes travel in schools, once one dogfish is hauled aboard via net or line, many more may follow. (The school has also probably run off the desired fish, and a new fishing location will have to be found.) A dogfish aboard a boat can be difficult to subdue and must be handled cautiously. In addition to its sharp teeth, it has two slightly venomous spines on its back, one in front of each fin. If one of the spines punctures flesh, a gland releases venom into a shallow groove along the spine. From there the poison flows into the victim's skin, resulting in a painful wound.

Although dogfish are eaten in Europe and other parts of the world, they have never caught on in North America as a culinary treat. At one time, however, their skin was sold for use as sandpaper, and they were also harvested for the high vitamin A content in their livers, but when other sources were discovered, the fishery deflated. Today, most dogfish caught are used not for their vitamins or tasty flesh but as preserved dissection specimens for premed students and school biology departments.

Like other sharks, spiny dogfish have remarkable sense organs that perceive water temperature, salinity, and pressure. The animals are also responsive to chemical "smells" in the water. A "lateral line" running the length of each side of the body is studded with sensitive hairs that recognize vibrations. Additional hairs in pit organs dispersed over the head help the shark home in on the abnormal swimming patterns of sick or injured fish. Like wolves and other high-level land predators, sharks help cull the weakest animals. The spiny dogfish's list of prey includes herring, sand lances, crabs, shrimps, smelts, squid, and octopus. They also take salmon, although perhaps only disabled ones.

Studies show that dogfish may make long migrations, and that when they school, they are segregated by gender. This may help the survival of the species, since the males are not around to eat new babies. The mothers become inhibited from eating shortly before the young are born.

Rather than shedding sperm and eggs into the water as do many fish, sharks mate more in the manner of mammals. The

SPINES IN FRONT OF
BOTH TOPMOST FINS

male inserts one or two claspers into the female (claspers were so named because biologists first thought they were used to hold females in place during mating), which release sperm, fertilizing the eggs internally. The female carries her offspring for almost two years—probably the longest gestation of any vertebrate. The mother does not continue to pass along nutrients to her young, however. Each hen-sized egg has its own large yolk sac from which the embryo takes nourishment; the mother provides protection and oxygen. The sharp spines of the developing young fish are covered with pads of tissue that protect the mother. Four to six babies are typically born from a single female. The long gestation ensures well-developed young; these "babies" are from eight to twelve inches long (the mothers are generally only four feet themselves) and are fully prepared to take care of themselves from birth.

A happy combination for spiny dogfish—well-developed young, a wide variety of food choices, and little predation by humans or other animals—results in a large population. That good fortune extends to surfers, swimmers, and divers in our waters: our most numerous shark is also one of the least dangerous ones.

Tufted Puffin

Latin name: *Fratercula cirrhata*

Description: 15 inches. Breeding plumage: white face; two feathery tufts, pale yellow and about 4 inches long, over eyes; bill mostly bright orange-red; body black. Winter plumage: face black; beak smaller and base of bill dusky brown; upper body black, lower sooty gray.

Habitat: Usually at sea, but on rock promontories and other nursery locations scattered along the coast during breeding season.

The stocky, colorful tufted puffin looks more like something made up by a stuffed-animal manufacturer than a real-life bird. When puffins are in their breeding plumage, the faces of both sexes become as starkly white as a clown's face paint, and each eyebrow sprouts a jaunty straw-colored feather tuft that droops over the back of the neck. Even their orange feet become more brightly colored than the pale salmon hues of winter.

We are far more likely to see puffins in their breeding costumes than in the duller plumage they wear half of the year because they are seabirds that come near shore only to breed. Even then, they usually don't get too close to people, preferring rocky offshore headlands, islands, and isolated coastal bluffs. Because their stubby wings have trouble lifting their bodies up into the air, these high outcroppings may allow them to launch more easily.

Puffins begin arriving at their breeding colonies each year around April and remain until August or September. During the mating season, their bills grow bigger, and the brown back portion of the upper bill turns a yellow that sets off the bright orange-red on the rest of the bill. (Like most birds' bills, the puffin's bill is a horny sheath of modified thick skin that is continuously sloughed off and replenished.)

In addition to impressing a mate, the puffin's bill serves to remove stones when digging an underground nest for its young. The bird's toenails dig into the earth, and the webbed feet help scoop and push the soil out of the burrow. The tunnel may be relatively shallow, ending after one foot, or it may extend five feet into the earth before ending in a chamber that is sometimes lined with grasses and feathers. Here the female lays her single egg. Both sexes apparently incubate the egg and also take turns brooding the chick once it has hatched. The off-duty parent leaves the breeding colony on frequent trips to find food.

Puffins eat mostly fish from six to eight inches long, including sand lances, smelt, sardines, herring, and perch, although they will also take squid, mollusks, and sea urchins. Early naturalists were puzzled by how a puffin parent managed to transport so many fish in its beak. They noted that a bird could carry up to six fish crosswise in its bill at one time, but they wondered how it managed to catch numbers two through six after it had its beak closed around number one. The answer is that the bird secures its first catches between its rough tongue and upper mandible, leaving the lower bill available to close on more prey. Apparently it can also catch prey first on one side of its bill and then on the other. Puffins dive and pursue fish below the surface, using their wings as paddles to fly underwater.

Because they are diurnal birds (active in the daytime), it's possible to spot puffins off Northwest shores. Look for grassy-topped outcroppings and watch for the furiously flapping birds arriving with food for their young. (They are usually silent, so you can't rely on their calls to alert you to their presence.) Perhaps because it looks so cuddly or clownish, the tufted puffin is one bird that just about everyone is happy to get a chance to see.

Marbled Murrelet

Latin name: *Brachyramphus marmoratus*

Description: About 10 inches; chunky body, short neck, stubby tail; winter plumage dark gray above, with white neck and underside; summer plumage brown above, with marbled brown-and-white neck and underside.

Habitat: Offshore ocean waters except in nesting season; nests in old-growth or mature second-growth forests up to 50 miles inland.

Back in the 1800s, the nesting habits of a small seabird, the marbled murrelet, confounded ornithologists. The Native people of the Northwest told curious explorer-naturalists that the murrelet nested in the forest. But that seemed implausible; after all, everyone knew that seabirds rear their young in crowded colonies on cliffs or outcroppings.

Generations of biologists continued the murrelet nest quest. Although a marbled murrelet was found nesting on a rock slide in Alaska in 1931, not a single ground nest could be found in Pacific Northwest coastal areas.

Tantalizing clues turned the searchers toward the forests. In 1953 a stunned murrelet—and fragments of an egg—came down with a large hemlock felled in British Columbia. The calls of marbled murrelets, which loggers recognized as those of "fog larks" could be heard in old forests. And chicks were occasionally found on forest floors.

Despite all the deliberate scientific searches, it wasn't until 1974 that the first aerial murrelet nest was accidentally discovered by a tree trimmer. He was five miles from the ocean and one hundred and fifty feet up in a Douglas-fir when he spotted the web-footed young bird crouching in a depression on a tree branch. It was so unlike any other chick he'd seen that he brought it down from the tree. The young bird was identified as a marbled murrelet, but it died within a few days. It would be more than a decade before the next nest was found, and not until 1989 that a tree nest with an adult incubating its egg would be located. The marbled murrelet's tree nests were the last nests found of any North American breeding bird.

Not only does this ocean-living bird nest in the forest, but studies indicate that it may require huge old trees with thick limbs. The single egg is laid in a moss-covered depression sheltered by an overhanging branch or perhaps a clump of mistletoe.

How did the marbled murrelet keep its nesting site a secret for so long? The answer lies not only in its location but also in the parents' stealth. The two take turns brooding their single egg, relieving each other only in the haziness of dawn or dusk. After the chick hatches, they feed it in darkness. Although their "fog lark" *keer* call can be heard in the forest, the birds are silent as they near the nest. Murrelets have been clocked flying at nearly sixty miles per hour; in the forest they hurtle at breakneck speed high above the forest floor, dodging trunks and branches in the dim light. These sneaky tactics, plus their camouflaging summer coloration (the *marbled* of its common name), make it extremely difficult to track the birds, even when researchers are observing a known nest.

There's good cause for the murrelet's furtiveness. Ravens and Steller's jays are among the young chick's worst enemies, especially in second-growth forests, which offer less cover. The larger birds can easily devour the nestling or even shove aside the brooding robin-sized parent to steal its egg. Should the young survive its predators and other perils including high winds, it still faces the daunting challenge of reaching the ocean.

The parents apparently urge their young to do this by simply never returning to the nest. After a few nights, the hungry chick relies on instinct. It leaps from the tree at dusk, never having flown before. This very first flight takes it to the ocean, where it must catch the fish previously supplied by its parents.

Habitat destruction seems to be the greatest threat to the murrelet. It survives in the Pacific Ocean only near coastal areas that still harbor old-growth trees or second-growth trees with old-growth characteristics. This once-abundant bird is now officially listed as a threatened species. Because of that protected status, the seabird that previously confounded ornithologists now confounds logging companies and many people who depend on logging for their livelihood.

Moon Jellyfish

Latin name: *Aurelia aurita*

Description: To 15 inches across, but usually smaller; whitish; saucer-shaped. Four horseshoe-shaped gonads visible on topside; females have yellowish gonads; males have lavender or pink gonads; immatures have white ones.

Habitat: Drifting just under the surface within a few miles of shore, occasionally in bays, estuaries.

Moon jellyfish bob near the surface of the ocean as if reluctant to sink too far away from the moon they were named after. This lovely, translucent, pulsing animal is the Pacific Northwest's most common jellyfish.

Washed up on a beach, a jellyfish quickly turns into an unrecognizable gelatinous blob. But in its element, a moon jelly is shaped something like a small umbrella, its rim scalloped by eight lobes. Short tentacles hang down from the lobes like fringe. The animal's mouth, in the center of the underside, is surrounded by four fluted, frilly oral arms.

Other large jellies depend on their tentacles, loaded with stinging cells

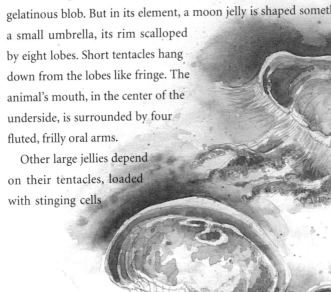

called nematocysts, to capture and subdue prey. The moon jellyfish employs a different feeding strategy. The upper side of its bell and its oral arms produce a sticky mucus that traps plankton, the tiny plants and animals that float near the ocean's surface. These are conveyed down the bell by small, waving, hairlike cilia. The oral arms regularly sweep around the rim of the bell, collecting the little munchies and transferring them to the mouth.

Although the moon jelly doesn't use its tentacles for capturing prey, they are loaded with nematocysts whose sting is mildly toxic to humans and can itch and aggravate for hours afterward. The nematocysts are independently triggered by contact or pressure, not through any deliberate effort on the jellyfish's part, so even after the animal is dead, its nematocysts can still fire. Like other jellies, dead or alive, swimming or beached, moon jellyfish should not be touched with bare fingers or prodded with bare feet.

In some years, they are washed up in large numbers onto broad sandy beaches. This is because their pulsing swimming style (they collect water by expanding the bell and then expel it by contraction) cannot compete with strong currents. If the jellyfish winds up too close to the beach, it is unable to travel against the shoreward march.

Moon jellies are seen especially in spring and summer, and occasionally fill a bay's waters in sudden, staggering numbers. Although the adult form is less likely to be seen the rest of the year, the immature form are always present in our waters. Young moon jellies are so different from their floating parents that for a long time the two forms were thought to be separate species. The moon jellyfish's curious reproductive system involves "alternate generations," where the young resemble the grandparent, not the parent.

The sperm and eggs of male and female jellyfish travel from the gonads into their stomachs, then to their mouths, and from there into the sea. Female moon jellies retain some of the eggs on their sticky oral arms, where they are protected as they are fertilized by the swimming sperm. Fertilized eggs become planulae, tiny larval creatures that swim using cilia and travel with the currents.

The planulae actively seek somewhere to attach themselves. Finding a suitable place, perhaps the underside of a floating dock, a pier piling, or a rock or shell on the sea bottom, the planula settles in, often with some of its peers. Each planula now develops into a polyp: it elongates and grows sixteen tentacles. The small polyps, protected from winter storms, live out their lives nabbing and eating small shrimplike organisms and other tiny animals. An individual can create identical clones by budding. A lump develops on the side of a polyp, grows larger, and then pulls off entirely, settling nearby. Although these additional polyps cannot bud, come springtime all the polyps, whether they formed from budding or from a planula, can create the next generation.

The polyps now grow longer, lose their tentacles, and develop grooves that encircle their bodies. As these furrows grow increasingly deeper, the polyps resemble a stack of saucers. The top "saucer" develops tentacles and breaks away from the others; the rest follow in turn. Each of these is a tiny medusa, or jellyfish. When they become adults, they will reproduce sexually as their grandparents did, creating planulae—which when mature will reproduce asexually to create medusas.

The medusas are the only form we usually see of this intriguing reproductive pattern, in which no individual produces young that resemble itself. And unfortunately, most of us only see dead, beached medusas, which scarcely resemble their living selves either—those lovely pale moons that orbit just beneath the water's surface.

Dungeness Crab

Latin name: *Cancer magister*

Description: Shell to about 9 inches at its widest; upper shell purplish or orangish brown, tan or grayish, undersurfaces lighter. Front edge of shell has 10 or so small, sawlike points.

Habitat: Estuaries, eelgrass beds, bays, around piers, wharfs, breakwaters, deep water to 600 feet.

In some winters the cast-off, molted shells of Dungeness crab are so numerous and obvious that many people become convinced the animals themselves are washing ashore, dead from pollution or some terrible disease. The confusion is understandable. The Dungeness crab population fluctuates wildly; years can pass with relatively few molts arriving on the beaches, while at other times hundreds of them are cast up to form long embankments on the sand. And because each molted shell is whole (although empty), it can appear that dead crabs are piling up.

All crabs molt in order to grow. Instead of the internal skeletons that soft-bodied animals like ourselves employ, they have hard outer exoskeletons. This shell protects them, but every so often crabs (like other crustaceans, or "crusty-bodied" creatures) must give up the safety of the confining shell so they can grow.

When it's time for the animal to molt, a crack develops along the rear edge of the crab's shell and the animal backs out, leaving the old exoskeleton neatly intact. Now the crab inflates itself by taking in water. It is making room, before its new shell hardens, for more growth to occur. The crab is now in the soft-shell stage, which means both that it is more vulnerable to predators and that if you catch one for your dinner its meat will be rather mushy and watery. Left alone, the shell will harden, and the animal will gradually become heavier and heavier as it grows to fit the new exoskeleton.

It is the synchronized molting of the male Dungeness crabs that sometimes becomes especially noticeable in the late winter months. The males all molt at once for a reason, and naturally that reason is sex. Crabs mate when the female is in the soft-shell stage, and the males need to be back in their hard-shell stage by then. The females' molt is not synchronized, but occurs throughout the spring and summer.

Because the males know when an adult female is preparing to molt, scientists speculate that she releases hormones in her urine. A male who tracks down such a female immediately embraces her. The two may remain for days in the clinch, belly to belly. Should she become restless during this tight courtship, the male soothes her by rubbing her shell with his claws. When the female is ready to molt, she informs the male by nibbling on his eyestalks. This causes him to loosen his grip so she can turn around. Still within the protecting embrace of his arms, she slips out of her old shell and into something more comfortable. After she pumps herself up, and perhaps her shell hardens a bit, the two finally mate. He releases sperm through special appendages into her reproductive openings. She will hold this sperm for several months in an abdominal receptacle until she is ready to lay her eggs. After mating, the male continues to clasp the female until her shell hardens and she is able to defend herself.

In late fall or early winter, the eggs are finally fertilized by the waiting sperm as they emerge. Throughout the winter months, the female carries the eggs with her, tucked up against her abdomen. The female's abdominal flap, which is like a modified tail, is different from the male's, and this is an easy way to determine a crab's sex: his flap is narrower and triangular, while hers is more U-shaped. The broader flap allows her to carry up to a million eggs. These develop into embryos, which are finally released in late winter or early spring.

The young go through a series of molts. By the time they resemble tiny crabs, about four months later, they seek the refuge of estuaries to continue molting and growing. As they near adulthood, they will have mastered the Dungeness crab lifestyle. They will avoid predators by burrowing backward in the sand so that only their eyes and antennae show. They will feed on small fish, marine worms, and small clams and abalones, chipping open the shells with their pincers. (Crabbers use turkey legs, dead fish, or some other animal flesh for bait.)

Three-year-old Dungeness are prepared to enter the adult crab world, and the males are ready to begin the synchronized late-winter molt in the offshore waters. Another generation of young Dungeness crabs leaves the sheltering estuaries, armed with their knowledge of crab survival skills—and drawn back to the ocean by the promise of soft-bodied sex.

Scallops

Latin name: *Hinnites giganteus, Chlamys hastata, Chylamus rubida*

Description: To 6 inches in diameter, depending on species; shell is fan-shaped with radiating ridges and furrows; two jutting "ears" near hinge; size and color vary according to species.

Habitat: Different species are found in deep water, just offshore, in large beds on seafloor, or attached to rocks in crevices and under boulders.

People don't expect much from shellfish—except perhaps a tasty meal. But apart from their culinary qualities, scallops, as bivalves go, are surprisingly alert little creatures. Among all the wide ocean's two-shelled animals, only scallops have eyes and can see. Their many eyes have lenses and retinas, and are a lovely shade of deep greenish blue. Although scallops are unable to perceive images, they can detect movement and changes of light and shadow. The eyes are located in a row lining the inside edges of both of the animal's shells, and they alternate

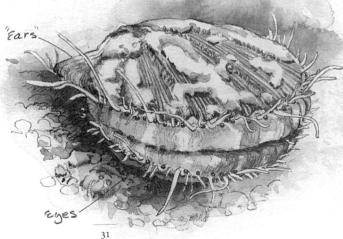

"Ears"

Eyes

31

with sensory tentacles that stretch out of the shell to gather additional information. A scallop's only blind spot is its hinge, where the shells join.

When they detect the presence of a sea star, most scallops don't just slam shut and hope the predator chooses someone else to pull apart. Instead, they leap into action. An offshore bed of scallops invaded by a sea star erupts into jet-propelled, clapping shells. Those employing the escape mechanism jump backward with a clap of their shells that expels water out the front. Those that opt to swim away repeatedly clap their shells, directing the gulps of water out small openings on either side of their hinges and moving jerkily forward. They look like swimming castanets, or, as has often been suggested, two jaws biting their way through the water.

Two common swimming scallops found in Pacific Northwest waters, the spiny pink and the smooth pink scallops (*Chlamys hastata* and *Chylamus rubida*), almost always have a helpful sidekick in their never-ending battle against sea stars. Encrusting sponges (*Myxilla incrustans* and *Mycale adhaerans*) often entirely cover the scallop's uppermost shell, the left one. (Scallops invariably lie on their right valve, which is more rounded than the left. This lifts them up off the seabed a bit, making it easier for them to keep an eye on things.)

The encrusting sponges help to repel sea stars by tactile camouflage. The predator's exploring tube feet discover inedible sponge rather than inviting scallop shell. Even if the star touches a bit of recognizable shell, it apparently finds it difficult to adhere its tube feet onto the sponge and so is unable to pull the shells apart. In this mutually beneficial relationship, the scallop also actively protects its protector. Should the sponge's predator, a nudibranch, get too close, the sponge gets to ride its galloping scallop far from danger.

Not all scallops are swimmers, however. The sedentary rock scallop (*Hinnites giganteus*) begins life like the free-roaming ones. Eggs and sperm released into the ocean water meet to create swimming larvae. The tiny creatures that manage to survive heavy predation eventually drop to the ocean floor and molt into baby scallops that resemble their parents. When it is between three-quarters and two inches long, the rock scallop finds a nice shell or rock to settle on and makes its permanent home. Its right side adheres to the rock, and as the scallop grows, its shell conforms to the irregular shape. The animal gradually loses the classic scallop shell design, although its youthful outline can be seen near the hinge. Once attached, rock scallops grow slowly and may take twenty-five years to reach their full size of five or six inches long.

Unlike many other shellfish, scallops lack a siphon. Scallops are filter feeders. They both feed and breathe by letting their shells gape open. In a neat bit of efficiency, the gills simultaneously draw oxygen from the water washing over them and strain microscopic food as well. Over the years, they transform those minuscule food organisms into yummy flesh that many creatures desire. In addition to sea stars, scallops' predators include octopuses, birds, fish, seals, mink, and of course, people. Unlike the other creatures, though, we humans usually eat only the round abductor muscle that holds the shells together—despite the fact that the rest of the animal is equally tasty. It's difficult to say what holds us back from enjoying the rest of the scallop—habit, ease of preparation . . . or maybe those disconcertingly blue eyes.

Salmon

Latin name: *Oncorhynchus* spp.

Description: From 40 to 58 inches long, depending on species; small fin on back, before tail fin. Different species have distinct colorations, as do males and females within a species; sea-run and spawning fish of the same species can also differ in color and body shape.

Habitat: Northeastern Pacific Ocean, estuaries, lakes, large rivers and small tributaries, depending on species and age.

Salmon are an ancient example of the circles and cycles embedded in the natural world. In the classic drawing of the salmon life cycle, curving arrows lead in a never-ending circle from round eggs to hatched young to oceangoing fishes to the mature, spawning adults that return to make the round eggs. And in most populations, the fish makes a round-trip journey, drifting down its natal tributary into larger and larger streams until it reaches the ocean, where it travels in a gyre that eventually brings it back to the river, into the streams, to the exact tributary of its birth, to spawn and die. These dead and dying fish return nutrients to the river, and, as their bodies are carried away by predators, to the lands surrounding the river. Some of these predators have become synchronized to bear their own offspring so as to take advantage of the prehistoric cycle; other animals, including some people, time their own annual migrations to prime catching and feeding areas.

There are five species of Pacific salmon, although it can seem like more because they have been given so many different common names. The five, from largest to smallest, are:

Chinook (*Oncorhynchus tshawytscha*), a.k.a. king, spring, black-mouth, tyee (those weighing over thirty pounds)

Coho (*O. kisutch*), a.k.a. silver

Sockeye (*O. nerka*), a.k.a. red, blueback, kokanee (a freshwater fish that never enters the ocean)

Pink (*O. gorbuscha*), a.k.a. humpback

Chum (*O. keta*), a.k.a. dog salmon

Jack salmon are early-maturing males that return to spawn before the rest of their age group; they can be chinook, coho, or sockeye. (There are also cases of early-maturing females called jills.) Two other Northwest fish species are classified as "salmonids," meaning that they are in the salmon family, but these are trout, not salmon. The two are cutthroat trout (*O. clarkii*) and the fish known as rainbow trout or steelhead (*O. mykiss*).

Chinook and coho are the most popular salmon for sport fishing but are the least numerous of the five species. The remaining three species support the commercial salmon fishing industry—especially the pink, which is the most abundant.

Many Northwesterners know that salmon faithfully return to the very stream in which they were hatched. Less appreciated, but no less amazing, is that each stock is uniquely suited to its own specific stream. (A stock is a population of fish defined by a unique behavioral, genetic, or physiological trait. For example, two stocks of the same species that spawn in the same river could be differentiated if one returns in August, while the second doesn't show up until October. Or the defining characteristic might be that one stock is immature upon arrival and has to wait to breed, while another stock arrives fully mature and prepared to spawn.) There are hundreds of stocks within each of the five salmon species, and some of these stocks are genetically distinctive. Their evolution has been shaped by the complexity of their particular home stream to the point where even some of the stocks that use the same stream at different times of the year are distinct from one another. This trait has allowed salmon to both maximize usage of each stream and minimize competition between stocks. However, for this same reason, any sudden massive change in a waterway (such as the building of a dam) can have profound effects on the stocks. Hatchery propagation can also endanger natural diversity because traits favored by humans (such as those that make fish easier to handle or raise) are unlikely to be beneficial outside the fish farm. Introduced hatchery fish that breed with wild ones may ultimately dilute the wild stock's ability to survive.

Despite the inconceivable multitude of salmon that once used virtually every waterway in the Pacific Northwest, despite the spiritual and physical connection between the fish and many Native tribes, and despite the economic importance and continued symbology of the salmon in the Northwest, wild salmon in this area may be forever lost. Already it is estimated that they have vanished from forty percent of their historic spawning streams.

The situation is so dire that in 1999 nine stocks of Pacific salmon were listed as threatened or endangered by the federal government. The implications of those listings affected more than seventy-two thousand square miles of waterways in Washington and Oregon and continue to demand not only changes from industries but changes in how virtually every Northwesterner uses water. Never before has the Endangered Species Act impacted so large, so heavily populated, and so urbanized an area, which includes Seattle and Portland.

It can be argued that the Northwest has an obligation to the salmon; it can also be said that we have an opportunity to show how citizens can rally to protect a species. After all, who better than Pacific Northwesterners to demonstrate individual environmental responsibility—and what fish more exemplifies the Northwest than its native salmon?

Common Murre

Latin name: *Uria aalge*

Description: About 17 inches; black back, white underneath; short tail; long, dark, pointed bill; narrow dark brown streak above adult's eye in winter.

Habitat: Ocean waters; nest on offshore cliffs during breeding season; also in Puget Sound during winter months.

I didn't know much about seabirds when I volunteered to help clean the ones caught in an oil spill off Grays Harbor, Washington, in December 1988. I was shown how to hold an alarmed bird's beak scissored between two fingers to avoid being stabbed, how to wield the water-piks and soft toothbrushes used to loosen the worst of the black gunk, and how to work the oil-cutting suds in between feathers. I was then handed a black bird and told that it was a murre. As the water sluiced away the stinky ooze, I was amazed to discover that the bird in my hands had a breast of startling white. This is how I learned that murres resemble penguins when not sodden with killing oil.

Common murres were particularly vulnerable to the oil spill. They feed by diving beneath the water surface and so became thoroughly coated with the oil. Also, because they are gregarious, a large segment of their population was affected. Other seabirds share these traits, but because murres are most numerous, they came into the hastily created cleaning center in staggering numbers.

In addition to their coloration, murres resemble penguins in other ways: their legs are positioned far back on their bodies, and they have an upright stance on land. Murres also flap their wings to "fly" underwater (but, unlike the flightless penguins, they can fly above the water too). The resemblance is not a familial one; the two kinds of birds are an example of convergent evolution. Faced with similar situations in either hemisphere, two entirely different species took similar evolutionary paths. Murres belong to a family called the alcids, which includes other penguinlike birds such as puffins, auklets, and murrelets.

Murres don't usually set foot on dry land until they are ready to nest. Then they converge in large numbers on ledges and cliffs, crowding together nearly shoulder to shoulder. They have no need of conventional nests because the parents take turns holding their large, lone egg on their webbed feet. Still, delicate eggs and precipitous cliffs would seem an unlucky combination. A clever adaptation prevents the eggs from rolling right off the ledges, however: a murre egg is noticeably pointed on one end and, when bumped, it pivots around on this small end in a tight circle.

Murre eggs are extremely variable in color. They can be green, pink, gray, white, brown, or blue and patterned with dark squiggles, streaks, or splotches. The designer eggs allow the parents to recognize their one and only in the crowded colony.

When the offspring hatches, both parents continue to tend it. For about three weeks they deliver small fish, one at a time, to their shrill, demanding chick. Then it's time for junior to take the plunge. Encouraged by the adults waiting below, the young murre boldly steps off its ledge, fluttering sometimes more than a thousand feet down to the water. Now the father apparently takes on sole parenting responsibility, teaching his only child how to fish and fend for itself.

Although murres eat some bottom fish and are known to dive to five hundred and fifty feet, their main prey is small schooling fish like herring and smelt, which they eat underwater. Their main predators are orcas and sea lions. And humans continue to have an impact on murre populations.

In the mid-1800s, millions of murre eggs were collected for food; today these birds are threatened by less direct means. Pesticides have been linked to reduced population figures and, as I learned at Grays Harbor, murres frequently comprise more than ninety percent of the seabirds killed in oil spills. Even those that survive the initial dunking may not survive all the handling needed to capture, clean, and eventually release them. Many birds die of shock. I later learned that of the ten thousand seabirds collected in the relatively small 1988 spill, nine thousand were dead or died while in captivity (statistics show that seventy-five percent of cleaned birds die); only one thousand survived the ordeal and were released.

There are two murres I remember most clearly from the scores I handled during those terrible, hectic days of cleaning. One was the first, with its bright white feathers suddenly revealed; the other was one who had endured the spill, the capture, the wait with all the other oiled seabirds, the force feedings, and nearly the entire rigorous, hourlong washing procedure, only to die in my hands as I rinsed away the last suds.

Sea Pen

Latin name: *Ptilosarcus gurneyi*

Description: To 20 inches long; bulbous base and fleshy stalk ending in featherlike structures; pale to bright orange.

Habitat: Estuaries, bays, offshore waters with soft bottoms.

A person confronted with a sea pen for the first time would be more apt to conclude it was related to the forest's ferns than the ocean's jellyfishes. Sea pens are one of those fantastic water creatures that look more like plants than the animals they truly are.

To make it a bit more confusing, a sea pen is not a single animal but a colony of many small individuals called polyps, or zooids. Different types of polyps do specific jobs on behalf of the colony. The body cavities of the polyps that make up the base of the sea pen connect with channels running the length of the colony and their mouth openings usher water in and out of the colony to ventilate it. If the sea pen is disturbed, or if it lives close to shore and a low tide occurs, the polyps can quickly release water. This causes the sea pen to shrink and helps it to sink into the soft sea bottom. When the danger passes or the tide returns, the polyps pump in water to reinflate the colony.

The top section of a sea pen has many side branches, each lined with hundreds of feeding polyps. Each of those polyps has eight tentacles armed with nematocysts, the same kind of stinging cells found in sea anemones (a close relative). Their sting doesn't penetrate human skin, but packs a powerful wallop to the tiny animals that are a sea pen's prey. The nematocysts also help defend against predators, especially sea stars and nudibranchs.

The tentacles also give the sea pen a fluffy, feathery look, and the name sea pen refers to the colony's similarity to an old-fashioned feather quill pen. Although it might seem like a sea pen is about as likely as a feather pen to move about under its own power, the aquatic version can change its location at will. If a site is unsuitable, the sea pen pulls its base, or peduncle, out of the mud and undulates its way to a better location. The sea pen requires a nice soft substrate of mud, sand, or a combination of each, to sink its peduncle into. It literally settles into its new location, embedding about half of the base.

Sea pens tend to live in groups, aligning themselves at an angle to the current to optimize feeding. Nudged by the water currents, the cluster of pens bends and moves like seaweed. The currents also help jettisoned sperm and eggs mix and mingle in a reproductive singles party. And a strong push of the current will sometimes cause the sea pens to bioluminesce. When stimulated (also by a diver's hand or the touch of an enemy) sea pens exude a slime containing luminescent particles that emit an impressive greenish light. The purpose of the light is not known, but it is speculated that it might be used to startle or even temporarily blind predators.

The sea pen turns out to have a surprising amount of talent: the ability to light up, move from place to place, bury itself when need be, and sting predator or prey. In the case of the sea pen, thousands of polyp heads work better than one.

By-the-Wind Sailor

Latin name: *Velella velella*

Description: 3 to 4 inches long; flat, oval, bluish body with short tentacles below and a small transparent, triangular sail above.

Habitat: Floats freely about the ocean but can be blown onto beaches, sometimes in huge numbers.

*f*or many years the by-the-wind sailor was thought to be a jellyfish and, like them, to be composed of a number of individuals forming a complex colony. Nowadays, scientists recognize that each sailor is a single individual and a hydroid, a type of cousin to the jellyfish. It has been said that unlike most hydroids, which settle to the bottom of the ocean and grow a stalk, by-the-wind sailors have instead settled at the surface and grown a float.

Velella velella (which, with its roller-coaster of v's and l's, is much more fun to say than "by-the-wind sailor") can be found far out in the ocean, on the high seas. Boaters have reported seeing huge offshore drifts of *Velella velella*, like tiny sailboats stretching from horizon to horizon. But most of us encounter this wayfaring animal when it is blown too close to shore and tossed up on the beach. It doesn't take long for the beached little creatures to dry out and die. After the fleshy parts have disintegrated, only the sailor's cellophane-like disk is left to blow across the sand.

The living creature's sail propels it when it is blown across the waters. Looking down on the animal from above, you can see that the sail isn't aligned straight down the middle. Instead, it is mounted diagonally, and depending on which direction it is canted, the animal is said to be either "right-handed" or "left-handed." The result is that, rather than going straight downwind, *Velella velella* sails at a forty-five-degree angle to the wind. The right-handed ones tack to the left; the left-handed ones tack to the right. Out on the open ocean, these creatures are sorted out by the wind, right-handed ones sailing in one direction and left-handed ones in the other.

Light, southerly winds usually blow the sailors away from Northwest shores. But a strong wind can cause the animals to spin and eventually be driven toward the beaches. Huge numbers of *Velella velella* sometimes land ashore after the first strong southerly or westerly winds in early spring.

By-the-wind sailors travel through all the temperate and tropical oceans of the world. Their disks are filled with chambers of air that keep them afloat, but should they turn over, they apparently have no way to right themselves and will die.

On the underside of the disk is the creature's mouth. Its fringelike tentacles are armed with stinging cells called nematocysts that stun small prey and then escort the prey to the mouth and shove it in. (The nematocysts are too small to harm humans.) Sperm or eggs exit *Velella velella* via the mouth, and some scientists suggest that the animal's tentacles harbor many young in different stages of development until the offspring are ready to travel on their own.

Beachcombers witness only the death of by-the-wind sailors. But during their lives, these animals, with their sails set right or left, are wayfarers that ride the waves to wherever the wind takes them.

rhinophores

gills

Sea Lemon

Nudibranchs (Sea Slugs)

Latin names: *Hermissenda crassicornis; Anisodoris nobilis*

Description: Most 1 to 4 inches long; those in deeper water may grow to 10 or 12 inches long; often with striking coloration and variously shaped appendages.

Habitat: In tide pools, eelgrass beds, mudflats, estuaries; around floats, docks, pilings; in shallow water near shore.

Nudibranchs need a good public relations firm. Marine textbooks regularly refer to these mollusks as the most beautiful animals in the sea, yet the little snails-without-shells are unknown or overlooked by most people. The term "sea slug" certainly doesn't help their image.

Nudibranchs (pronounced "nudie-branks") are downright gaudy. They come in many colors, including lemon yellow, orange-red, and rosy pink; they can be sprinkled with black, outlined in frosty white, or streaked with electric blue. They might be striped, spotted, mottled, or all one hue. Some sport color combinations that shriek to be noticed, while others match their background so perfectly as to be nearly invisible.

Nudibranchs come in wildly fanciful shapes, too. Sensory tentacles called *rhinophores* that arise from the front or back of the animal can be conical, feathery plumes, or spires. The basic slug-body shape might be adorned with a circular tuft of gills at the back end, or entirely covered with projections called *cerata*. The cerata can be blunt and finger-shaped, wide and spade-shaped, or thin and pointy like thorny branches.

Over one hundred and seventy species of nudibranchs have been described along the Pacific Coast. The most common one in the Northwest is *Hermissenda crassicornis,* sometimes called the opalescent nudibranch. Its body is a translucent white with a bright orange line running down the back. Blue lines (sometimes a brilliant neon blue) run from the tentacles down either side of the orange line and also streak along the margins of the animal. Finger-shaped cerata cover the nudibranch's back, waving in the currents and with the animal's movements; each is usually a deep orange or brown, ending with a ring of bright orange and a white tip.

The cerata perform several functions for the nudibranch. Branches of the liverlike digestive gland run up inside them. They are also used for respiration, taking the place of gills used by other sea creatures (the name "nudibranch" translates to "naked gills"). The cerata are also used in defense. Many nudibranchs feed on animals such as anemones, which are armed with stinging cells called nematocysts. For some reason (perhaps the slime they exude protects them), the sea slugs are not injured or deterred by these harpoonlike cells. They simply gobble down the nematocysts along with the rest of the animal; the stinging cells are then sorted inside the nudibranch's body and migrate up into the cerata. The sea slug thus becomes armed with the weapons of its prey. Some species of nudibranchs can also lose cerata to an enemy, make an escape, and then grow more a few days later. Others employ chemical weapons, releasing sulfuric acid or toxins.

In *Anisodoris nobilis,* often called the sea lemon (shown on preceding page), the cerata are replaced by a flowery white plume of gills that surrounds the animal's anus on the rear upper side; the rest of the body is covered with tiny bumps. The sea lemon is bright yellow to orange and speckled with black. Like most nudibranchs, it is a fussy eater and feeds exclusively on sponges.

Nudibranchs are hermaphrodites (each individual has both male and female sex organs). Some species are male when young and become female as they grow older, but most species are both genders simultaneously. When two mate, each usually gives and receives sperm. Later, each will lay eggs in coils or rippling curtainlike masses, depending on the species.

With their enticing coloration, varied shapes, and interesting sex life, nudibranchs should be far more popular than they currently are. If they just had the correct packaging (including a catchy slogan—something like "Nudibranchs: the mermaid's lapdog"), pretty little sea slugs could become the darlings of the coast.

Sea Cucumber

Latin name: *Parastichopus californicus*

Description: To about 16 inches long; about 3 inches in diameter; tubular animal with prominent fleshy warts; usually dark red with orange, also brown above and yellow below.

Habitat: Low rocky tide pools or just offshore; also on sandy bottoms in deep ocean.

Not many of the world's animals could be appropriately named after a vegetable, but the sea cucumber's name fits it nicely. A sea cucumber (some smaller species are called "gherkins") looks more like a salad bar offering than like its closest relatives, which are sea stars, sand dollars, and sea urchins.

The giant or California sea cucumber is the most common species in the Northwest, and also the largest. It moves around, when it needs to, by means of three rows of small tube feet lining its flattened underside. Other tube feet have become fleshy pointed bumps on its upper surface, and still others have been modified into feeding tentacles that surround the cucumber's mouth, located at one end of its body. These white tentacles branch and branch again into plumelike structures that are often compared to mop heads.

The mop heads wave about, collecting small organisms on their sticky mucus surfaces, or swab detritus from the sand or mud. When the oral tentacles are coated with food, the cucumber does what any child with sticky fingers would: it inserts the tentacles one by one into its mouth and scrapes off the delectable items.

These tentacles, when extended, also reveal which end of the cucumber is the front end. If the oral tentacles aren't visible, it's still possible for an attentive observer to tell which way the animal is facing because it breathes through its anus, regularly taking in big gulps of water that circulate throughout its body. The anus opens into a chamber called the cloaca, which divides into branches that reach throughout the creature. This "respiratory tree" carries oxygenated water throughout the body. A short time after sucking in the water, the cucumber forcibly expels the deoxygenated water and takes in another refreshing gulp.

The cloaca often becomes a rooming house for small creatures that enter through the sea cucumber's anus and, apparently liking the accommodations, take up residence. Various flatworms, small crabs, and snails are said to take refuge from the harsh outside world, protected from their predators and collecting their own food as it is drawn into the cucumber with each breath. Some are commensals, which do no harm to the host, while others are parasites, which in some way live off the energy of the cucumber.

Freeloaders are routinely evicted, however. For any number of reasons, a sea cucumber will eviscerate, or eject its own internal organs out of its body, usually through the anus. By contracting, the animal squeezes the water inside itself, exerting pressure that forces out the organs, including the intestine and respiratory tree. The cucumber does this in response to danger, perhaps in an attempt to entice the predator with its offal while the rest of the animal makes its getaway. But it also appears to do this seasonally, in the fall, perhaps to rid itself of internal parasites. This is also the cucumber's standard response to changes in water temperature or fouled water. The lack of internal workings doesn't seem to hinder the creature, and it regrows them within a few months.

The giant sea cucumber, like most sea cucumbers, has separate sexes. Ova or sperm are released from the mouth in large quantities. The animals probably gather together in groups to ensure a better fertilization rate.

Although the swimming young are fair game for any number of hungry creatures, adult sea cucumbers seem to have few enemies. The multi-armed sunflower star might take some, and gulls have been seen eating beached cucumbers. But the animal's skin reportedly contains holothurin, a bad-tasting toxin that deters most potential predators.

Human palates are undeterred, however. The sea cucumber's internal muscles are considered a delicacy, especially in China and the South Seas. In meeting the demand abroad, there is concern that these creatures may be overfished in the Pacific Northwest and elsewhere. There can be no doubt that the human appetite is voracious, when it extends even to the warty, uninviting sea cucumber.

Harlequin Duck

Latin name: *Histrionicus histrionicus*

Description: 12 inches. Male: blue-gray with chestnut-brown flanks; large patch of white on head in front of eyes, other smaller patches on head; white streaks and other random patches on body; from a distance, plumage appears dark with bright white markings. Female: brown with lighter belly, three small white patches on head.

Habitat: Rough waters, including heavy surf along rocky coasts or turbulent mountain rivers.

My friends and I stood on an outcropping near the ocean's edge, training our binoculars on a small group of ducks riding the rocking water. It was hard to get a clear view of them because they kept disappearing between the bobbing waves. After a couple of glimpses of bold white on dark plumage, we decided they were harlequin ducks and went back to inspecting the crowded tide pools at our feet.

Ten days later, and nearly one hundred and fifty miles inland, I raised my binoculars to identify a pair of ducks on the far side of a rushing mountain river. Bold white on dark plumage. Really? I hastily consulted my field guide. Yes, harlequin ducks again.

What were these sea ducks doing on a rollicking river on the flank of the Cascade Mountains? Incredibly, they were there to breed. Pacific harlequins leave the ocean and travel many miles inland to mate; they nest as far east as Wyoming.

A rock offered shelter from the cold early May wind, and I hunkered down beside the river to watch the two ducks. Bucking the fast current, they repeatedly dove beneath the surface to feed. At the coast, harlequins brave the surf to feed on marine organisms like crabs, barnacles, chitons, and limpets, along with a few small fishes like sculpins. Here, they were after insect nymphs and larvae, like those of caddisflies, mayflies, and stone flies. Like the American dipper, another bird of rushing, frothing waters, the harlequin duck actually walks along the stream bottom, searching among the rocks and cobbles for its prey.

Perhaps the couple I watched already had a nest nearby, tucked among boulders or well hidden under streamside shrubbery. The female usually lays six to eight creamy eggs in a grass- and down-lined nest. Like a migrating salmon, a female returns to the stream of her birth at breeding time. She brings home with her a male she has bonded with back at the coast, and the two may form a long-term relationship. Nevertheless, once all the eggs have been laid and the female begins to incubate them, the male leaves her and travels back to the ocean, most likely following the river. Once there, he will join a large group of his male cronies and molt.

After about a month of incubation the babies hatch, and the female soon leads them to the river's edge. Unlikely as it seems, the downy young negotiate the foaming waters and quickly learn how to dive in search of food. They must survive many dangers if they are eventually to see the Pacific Ocean. Predators such as mink take their toll, as do high waters and cold weather. And even before her ducklings can fly, the mother takes off for the coast herself. Biologists speculate that, like her mate, she must get there before molting begins (which temporarily renders her flightless). After they fledge, the juveniles follow their instincts—and their birth stream—all the way to the ocean.

Because these birds require two different habitats, they end up in an environmental double whammy. The harlequin duck population is reduced by modern dangers as diverse as oil spills in the ocean and dams on the rivers, as well as by the ubiquitous dilemma of habitat loss. It appears that harlequin duck numbers, in the face of so many divergent pressures, are decreasing.

But in those waters that we haven't yet tainted or tamed, you can still find the dramatic harlequin duck, reveling in the rolling waves.

Scoters

Latin names: *Melanitta perspicillata* (surf scoter); *M. nigra* (black scoter);
M. fusca (white-winged scoter).

Description: 20 inches; plump, stocky body; short neck; male's bill has a hump near base; males are mostly or all black, depending on species; females are brownish.

Habitat: Offshore in wintertime; occasionally seen feeding at mussel-coated pilings or close to shore during high tides.

Scoters are hardy ducks, built not for dabbling in puddles or ponds but for diving in ocean waters. Compared to mallards or other dabblers, scoters seem downright beefy. Three kinds of scoters overwinter in Pacific Northwest waters: surf, black (formerly called "common"), and white-winged.

Surf scoters are aptly named. Undaunted by seething seas, this duck forages in breaking waves. Like the other scoters, it eats mollusks, crustaceans, and aquatic insects, and in spring favors the abundant herring eggs. One of its favorite mollusks seems to be the edible (blue) mussel, which it will procure by venturing near dock pilings or close to shore. With a characteristic little lunge, the scoter dives down and uses its formidable beak to wrench a mussel from its bed. Scoters are so tough (or at least their gizzards are) that they eat the mollusks whole, without bothering to shell them.

These sea ducks sometimes raft together in large numbers over mussel beds, and a rafting group occasionally synchronizes its movements, diving to feed and returning to the surface together. They may do this as a way to thwart thieving gulls: for all their bulky, tough-guy image, scoters can be intimidated by gulls (especially the glaucous-winged) into giving up their catch. Surfacing simultaneously may give more scoters the chance to finish their meal in peace.

Although surf scoters are the most numerous scoters found along Northwest coasts, both the black and white-winged are sighted as well. You may see all three species mingling, but the male black scoter is especially easy to identify because it is the only all-black duck found in Pacific Northwest waters.

The Pacific Northwest coastline is the winter feeding grounds of the scoters. Come nesting time, many will go to northern Canada's interior to lay their eggs. Although the males escort their mates to the traditional nesting grounds, they abandon the females shortly after the eggs are laid. Scoter nests, usually located near water, contain from five to nine eggs, depending on species. Little is known about the habits of the surf scoter, but females of the other two species incubate their eggs for about a month, and may continue to brood the small young at night after they hatch. The white-winged female occasionally lays her eggs in the nest of another duck mother, who hatches and raises the extra young along with her own.

Both the black and white-winged scoters' broods occasionally form "creches": the young separate from their parents to form a group supervised by only a few females. White-winged scoter broods numbering over one hundred and fifty chicks may be attended by only one to three hens. Presumably, raising young in a gang bestows some survival advantage. Creches occur only in areas where the nests are relatively close together.

Whether they grow up tended by mom or within a group of their peers, the young are initiated into scoter society. They learn how to dive and which foods are best (mussels!), and they learn how to get their increasingly heavy bodies airborne.

Although other types of ducks can spring directly up from their ponds or pools, scoters must beat their wings and run across the water surface. Their sturdy bodies require a greater effort to achieve lift-off, but that burliness is what allows scoters to live on the big pond.

Pacific Halibut

Latin name: *Hippoglossus stenolepis*

Description: To over 8 feet long; diamond-shaped body dark on upper side and light on lower; both eyes on same side of the body; slightly forked tail fin.

Habitat: Near or on bottom in deep water along the continental shelf to shallower water closer to shore, depending on season and individual's age.

Halibut grow to such immense proportions that, when taken aboard ships, they've killed and maimed people with their thrashing tails. Females can grow to nearly five hundred pounds and almost nine feet in length; males are half that length and generally not over one hundred pounds. (Most halibut caught locally are juveniles that average a more reasonable thirty-five pounds.) The fighting spirit of halibut challenges those who sport-fish, and its substantial, delectable meat makes the commercial halibut fishery one of the most valuable on the Pacific Coast.

A behemoth female may release as many as four million eggs during spawning, which occurs in deep ocean water. The young that develop are similar to other fish; they are symmetrical and have one eye on each side of their heads. But a halibut makes a strange transformation on its way from fry to adult fish. When it is still quite small, the left eye gradually migrates over the snout to pair up with the eye on the right side of the head. (Only rarely does the right eye migrate to the left side.) The animal's skull twists correspondingly to allow this, and some cartilage is reabsorbed so it doesn't block the eye's movement. The halibut's nostril also migrates, and its mouth twists to the right side. Meanwhile, the young fish begins to swim at a steadily increasing tilt, and its left side pales as its right darkens. By the time all its changes are complete, the halibut sinks to the bottom, prepared to take up life as a flatfish.

In its larval stage, a halibut feeds on plankton. As it grows, it seeks out smaller fish and shrimplike organisms. The greater its girth, the larger the fish it takes. Unlike other flatfish, such as sole and flounder, which generally live sedentary lives covered up by sand waiting for prey to come to them, the halibut is an active fish. It will chase after cod, pollock, and rockfish, as well as fish not found on the bottom such as herring and sand lance. A halibut will also take on an octopus or squid, as well as crabs and clams. Smaller flatfish, including other halibut, are also on its meal list.

Halibut are strong swimmers. Like other fish, they swim with an undulating rhythm of the whole body, except that halibut are oriented horizontally rather than being upright. They can travel great distances: fish tagged in the Bering Sea have been caught over two thousand miles away, off the coast of Oregon. Adult halibut undertake a much smaller, seasonal migration. In summer they frequent relatively shallow, coastal feeding grounds, and in winter they move to the deeper waters on the edge of the continental shelf to spawn. The sexes mature at different rates. Although females grow larger and faster, they generally mature later: most males reach sexual maturity at eight years old, and most females at twelve. Both sexes may live up to forty years.

Their size, their strength, and their bottom-hugging life all protect halibut to some degree from predation. They are occasionally eaten by marine mammals, but few fish would attempt such a meal. No doubt humans are their greatest predators, but even these adversaries know that halibut are a potentially dangerous fighter. Some people are so wary of a large halibut that they prefer to shoot the fish while it is still in the water rather than risk bringing it aboard still alive and kicking.

feeding tentacles

foot

Dentalium

Latin name: *Antalis pretiosum* (formerly *Dentalium pretiosum*)

Description: 1 to 3 inches long; slender, white shell with fine rings, slightly curved, wider at bottom than top.

Habitat: Saltwater, in gravel or sandy mud just offshore to 500 feet deep.

Dentalium's Latin species name, *pretiosum*, translates as "precious" or "valuable." This seems an odd designation for a small, obscure mollusk that spends its life buried in offshore sediment—unless you know its history. Dentalia, also known as Indian money tusks, were once as good as gold. These shells were the principal medium of exchange along the Pacific Coast for an estimated twenty-five hundred years.

Native people once brought bartering items from their various regions—abalone shells, mountain-sheep horns, canoes, slaves, or whale and seal oil—to trading sites like those along the Columbia River. The Nootka (from what is now Vancouver Island) brought dentalia, strung on thin lines of deer sinew. The finest and largest shells were reserved for their wealthy chiefs, but about forty two-inch shells could be strung on one line that was as long as the distance between a man's outstretched arms. Some researchers suggest that one such six-foot strand was worth a slave. One-inch shells were considered less valuable but were also used in trade.

Dentalia were worn as decoration, and wearing a strand meant that a man had his money at hand should he decide to barter or gamble. The shells were also used in payment to shamans and to adorn the dead.

Although dentalia can be found along the coast from Alaska to Baja California, the early traders may not have realized this because the shells were apparently harvested only at select, secret sites off Vancouver Island and a few places farther north. It's understandable that these small burrowing creatures could remain undiscovered in offshore beds. The surprising thing may be that the Nootka found them in the first place.

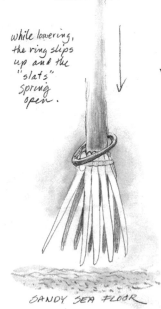

water level

while lowering, the ring slips up and the "slats" spring open.

SANDY SEA FLOOR

The Nootka probably used various harvesting methods, but the usefulness of one particular ancient device was debated for some time in the scientific community. This implement resembled a broomstick: a number of slender wooden slats were attached to one end of the pole, which was ten feet or longer; a ring of cedar-bark rope encircled the slats, holding them close together, and rocks were used to weigh it down to the sea bottom. In 1991, researchers built a replica of this tool and tested it in Kyuquot Sound on Vancouver Island. They positioned their boat over a known bed of dentalia and, with watching divers below, dropped the harvester into the water. As it went down, the force of the water raised the cedar ring up off the slats. The slats separated and, as they landed in the bed, several dentalia were pinned between the slats. When the device was pulled upward, the cedar ring slipped back down to hold the slats together, securing the shells. No one now doubts the tool's effectiveness.

Oblivious to the worth people may or may not assign to them, dentalia continue their quiet offshore lives. They spend their adulthood burrowed into the sea floor, pointy end up. Each tapered shell contains a mollusk with a foot for digging and a mouth for eating. Dozens of sticky threadlike tentacles reach out of the wider bottom opening, searching for minute pieces of plant or animal food. Larger pieces are rasped with a file-like radula into finer bits. Dentalia themselves are savored by various creatures, including ratfish and crabs. A tiny marine hermit crab may use a devoured animal's empty shell as a mobile home.

Dentalia are a kind of tuskshell (so called because they resemble miniature elephant tusks). The genders are separate in tuskshells, and in season females release eggs and males release sperm, which unite to form swimming larvae. The young eventually settle, sometimes far from their parents, and dig in to begin their sedentary lives.

Although the people of the Pacific Northwest may now place their collective faith in discs of metal and pieces of paper, it will take hundreds of years longer before modern money outlasts the span of time during which dentalia were valuable.

Bull Kelp

Latin name: *Nereocystis luetkeana*

Description: Usually grows 60 to 70 feet long but can be 100 feet;
a single long, slender stem ends in a bulb 4 to 6 inches in diameter from which
grow a number of straplike blades; olive-green overall.

Habitat: Off the coast in beds, at depths of 15 to 75 feet;
holdfasts require a rocky sea bed.

Every winter heaps of bull kelp pile up on Northwest beaches like huge tangled skeins of yarn. This seaweed is an annual plant that dies each year, so the seasonal storms easily tear it from its moorage. The bull, bullwhip, or ribbon kelp is a common seaweed found from Alaska to Northern California, and is easily identified. A long, slender, hollow stem, or stipe, leads to the bulbous float with its four groups of long, flat, ribbonlike blades. What appears to be the "roots" of the plant is in fact its holdfast—a fitting name for an attachment that is sometimes strong enough to carry the kelp's anchoring rock up onto the beach along with the plant itself. (Unlike the roots of a land plant, the holdfast does not gather nutrients.)

One of the largest of seaweeds, bull kelp can grow to over seventy feet in its single summer growing season. It lives just offshore, stretching up from the rocky bottom to bob its bulb on the water's surface. The hollow bulb contains a relatively large amount of carbon monoxide and some other gases that, by displacing water in the bulb, cause it to float. Looking like a windsock's streamers in a stiff wind, the bulb's radiating fronds wave in the ocean currents, gathering energy from the sun.

Like most seaweeds, bull kelp has alternating methods of reproduction. The asexual kelp plants produce chocolate-brown patches on their blades at the end of summer. These patches are made up of spores, and it is estimated that a single plant can produce a staggering three trillion seven hundred billion spores in one season. Few will survive. Once released from the kelp in late summer or autumn, the spores swim downward and settle on the ocean floor. This second generation grows into microscopic plants that are either male or female. Unlike their parent plant, they will reproduce sexually by producing sperm or eggs. Sometime during the winter the sperm swim to the eggs and fertilize them, resulting in a plant that grows into the familiar size and shape of bull kelp. The microscopic generation sandwiched between the larger-sized generations ensures the plants' survival in turbulent winter waters. It also means that the kelp we see this winter is the "grandchild" of the kelp we saw on the beaches last winter.

Despite its quirky reproductive methods, the bull kelp is an upstanding citizen in the offshore community. Kelp forests have been compared to lush land forests; they have understory and overstory plants and house a huge number of animals. The undulating groves provide habitat and safe harbor for dozens of fish and invertebrate species (animals without backbones, such as chitons, crabs, and nudibranchs). These attract larger fish and birds that feed on them; great blue herons sometimes use kelp floats as fishing platforms.

Animals that feed directly on bull kelp include the kelp crab and various nudibranchs. The red sea urchin is the most voracious among these herbivores, and thousands of them sometimes converge on a kelp forest, nibbling at their bases and effectively clear-cutting huge areas. There is some evidence that sea otters keep populations of urchins in balance so that kelp forests are not decimated. (Sea otters were eliminated from Washington and Oregon coasts for their fur, and have been reintroduced in Washington waters.)

Once cast ashore, often in a twisted mass like olive-green spaghetti noodles, the kelp is eaten by beach hoppers and other small scavengers. These little herbivores are not the only creatures who enjoy the taste of kelp; people sometimes gather the fresh hollow stipe of the seaweed to make pickles, and these reportedly taste excellent. The life of a bull kelp may be short, but the plant manages to get a tremendous amount of growth, reproduction, sheltering, and feeding of small animals into its one year.

Tides

The moon does more than cast a lovely, romantic glow on the ocean. As it travels in its orbit, that hypnotic eye pulls the water toward itself, raising and lowering the pulse of tides around the world.

It's the gravitational pull of the moon that holds the ocean in sway. (That same pull also exerts its influence on the land and on other objects on the Earth's surface, including people.) As the moon passes overhead, objects are drawn toward it, and the larger and less solid the object, the more obvious this is. The immense and utterly fluid ocean responds by rising up in a massive bulge beneath the moon. As the moon travels, the location of the bulge shifts to follow it. This heaping of water is undistinguishable in the open ocean, but reveals itself as high tide at the shoreline.

So far, so good. But consider that there are *two* high tides a day (as well as two low tides). As the moon pulls the water on one side of the Earth, a similar bulge occurs on the opposite side (scientific explanations for that second bulge differ, but have to do with the Earth's centrifugal force or the Earth's own attraction to the moon). At any rate, as the planet rotates on its axis, the coast experiences both of the high tides as well as the low tides situated between them (the extra water that goes into the high tide bulges has to come from somewhere—it is drawn from the areas of low tide).

But not all tides are created equal. One high tide is higher than the other, and one low tide lower than the other. The levels of the tides also vary from day to day because the tilt of the Earth's axis results in the moon traveling higher or lower in the sky, with its bulge of water faithfully following it.

Our sun also exerts a gravitational tug on the tides. Although the moon is puny compared to the sun (which is millions of times larger), it has more than twice the sun's gravitational pull because it is so much closer to Earth. Twice a month (during the full and new moons), the sun, the Earth, and the moon are arrayed in a straight line in space. Then the gravitational pulls of moon and sun are also aligned, resulting in a greater difference than usual between high and low tides. These are called spring tides. And twice a month (during the moon's first and third quarters), the sun and moon form a ninety-degree angle with Earth. Now the pull of the sun somewhat negates that of the moon, resulting in less of a difference than usual between high and low tides. These are called neap tides.

That's the basic outline, but other competing influences also determine the timing and levels of a particular area's tides. These include the shape of the shoreline, the slope of the beach, the depth of the water, winds, currents, and coastal storms. In addition, inertia and friction contribute to lag time, so that spring tides generally occur two or three days after a full or new moon; likewise, there is a lag of several hours between the time the moon passes overhead and the maximum tidal effect results.

Happily, beachcombers don't have to figure out all these variables themselves. Tide tables, usually adjusted for local conditions, are available at bait-and-tackle shops, sporting goods stores, dive shops, and marinas. Tidal information is also supplied in coastal newspapers.

Although observing beach life can be enjoyable at any time, you'll see more organisms if you time your visit to match low tides, especially the low spring tides. Just remember to watch out for the inevitable return of the waves, as the enthralled bulge rolls back in your direction.

Sand Dollar

Latin name: *Dendraster excentricus*

Description: About 3 inches across; nearly circular, flattened body; living animal is gray, black, brown, or purplish and covered with tiny spines; dead ones bleach white.

Habitat: Coastal beaches, in sandy beds running parallel to shoreline.

When my friend Diane visited from Ohio, she wanted to see the ocean. But when we arrived on the sandy beach that early spring day, it was a miserable place. Clammy fog and shrill wind had driven most other visitors from the beach. We gamely removed our shoes anyway and immersed our toes in the frigid water so Diane could say she'd waded in the Pacific. That accomplished, we were ready to go somewhere warm—when we spotted the sand dollars.

There were five of them, in faded shades of green and lavender. The bridesmaids' hues surprised us, especially Diane, who had seen only dead white ones. A recent storm must have carried the living sand dollars up onto the beach from their beds beyond the breakers. Diane and I picked them up for a closer look. Holding them on our open palms, we could feel their slight movement. Their undersides were covered with slowly moving short spines that looked like animated terrycloth. Using these spines, sand dollars are able to travel about and to bury themselves under sand. My landlocked friend's excitement over our unexpected find was contagious. The beach suddenly didn't feel quite so cold, and, fortified, we returned the circular animals to sand and turned into the wind for a long stroll down the beach.

The five-petaled design on the top of the sand dollar reveals its kinship to sea stars and sea urchins; all can be divided into five equal parts. Sand dollars breathe via tube feet, which they extend through holes along the margins of the petals. Though its gender is not obvious to the beach-comber, a sand dollar is either a male or a female. Sex cells are released from five pores located where the five petals come together. The spawning of one sand dollar in a colony triggers the others to release clouds of sperm and eggs. A fertilized egg develops into a swimming larva, which eventually settles when it finds just the right spot and develops into an adult.

A sand dollar's mouth is on its underside, near the center. The living animal has five triangular jaws, whose tips can just be seen. If you break open the white test (exoskeleton) of a dead animal, you'll see the five little V-shaped pieces, which some people say resemble flying birds. Sand dollars eat minute particles such as diatoms and bits of detritus. They may plow through the sand, ingesting as they go, or dig partially down into the sand until they stand upright on edge. (Young sand dollars sometimes selectively ingest the heaviest sand particles to act as a sort of weight belt and help anchor them in place.) Regiments of upright sand dollars parallel the shoreline, all leaning at the same angle, in the direction of the current.

On the underside of the animal, small beating hairs on the terrycloth-like spines create a slight current that draws in food particles. The particles catch on mucus exuded by the spines and flow toward the mouth via grooves. Like streams joining larger rivers, these branching grooves join larger channels that lead directly to the central mouth. These can be clearly seen on the bottom side of sand dollar tests, as can the small hole of the anus, located near the margin.

Sand dollars can sense the presence of certain sea stars and react to the enemy by burying themselves in the sand. They also do this in response to ocean storms, but as Diane and I discovered, they are sometimes washed ashore regardless. The surprising bridesmaids' colors we saw probably indicated that the animals were dying. As we walked the length of the beach, we found many more sand dollars, living and dead. When we left that day, Diane and I each carried a few of the white ones home with us, as souvenirs of a warming walk on a cold Pacific beach.

Lewis's Moon Snail

Latin name: *Polinices lewisii*

Description: Large, rotund shell to 5 inches high, with one large whorl at base and smaller whorls making a spiral; yellowish white to brownish gray; body when extruded covers lower part of shell.

Habitat: Protected beaches, bays, mud flats, and salt marshes, especially where sand is mixed with mud; to 160 feet offshore.

For many years naturalists were puzzled by the sand-encrusted rubbery "collars" they found on the beaches. Even Jack Calvin, one of the authors of the classic seashore guide *Between Pacific Tides*, admitted to having been confounded by them. As the book points out, moon snail egg cases look like "discarded rubber plungers of the type plumbers use to open clogged drains."

Lewis's moon snails and their odd egg cases appear on sheltered Pacific Northwest beaches between April and September, especially during May and June. The sexes are separate, and fertilization occurs during copulation. The female later lays her egg case just offshore or on the intertidal

drill hole

region of the beach. She extrudes as many as half a million minute eggs, embedded in a jellylike material. As the egg mass leaves her body, it is covered on either side with a protective coating of sand and mucus, making a sort of crusty egg-and-jelly sandwich. The growing gelatinous mass inches around the moon snail's body, encircling her and taking its characteristic collar shape from the "foot" of her body. When the case is completed, the snail moves out from under it. The resulting rubbery ring holds up for the next six weeks or so as the embryos within it develop. During a high tide, the covered cases on the beaches finally crumble and the larvae are carried away on the currents.

Eventually the young settle and begin to grow the beautifully round shells, reminiscent of the full moon, that earned them part of their common name. Both the common and the scientific name honor Meriwether Lewis, of Lewis and Clark fame, who carried specimens of the shell back East.

The Lewis's moon snail is the largest species of moon snail and also the largest intertidal snail in the Pacific Northwest. Its big, fleshy foot rises up to overlap the lower part of its shell, and it seems impossible the thing could completely fit back inside. But it can. Unlike other mollusks that extend their feet by inflating blood sinuses, the moon snail expands by pumping in seawater, which it can also release through perforations along the margin of its foot. A retracting

egg case

moon snail squeezes out water like a sponge, and a person who picks up and disturbs a moon snail is liable to get a surprise soaking. Like a magician's trick in reverse, the wrung-out snail fits entirely into its shell, and even closes the door behind it with a special hard section of the foot called the operculum.

Except during the breeding season, a moon snail spends much of its time under the sand rather than on top of it. The animal plows through the substrate, sometimes with the top of the shell just breaking the surface, in search of clams. Although vegetarian when very young, by the time it is an adult the moon snail is a carnivorous predator. It especially seems to relish clams, but also eats snails (including smaller moon snails), mussels, and oysters.

The moon snail has two basic means of attacking its hard-bodied prey. One is to simply wrap its huge foot around the shellfish and wait it out. The smaller animal, unable to extend its siphon, will eventually suffocate. Alternatively, the snail might drill its way through the victim's shell. Using its rasping, file-like radula and a shell-softening chemical secretion, the snail gradually wears a precise, round hole through the shell. After breaking through, the moon snail feasts on the soft animal inside by extending a long tubular feeding organ, the proboscis, into the shell and tearing up the interior flesh with its radula.

The mighty size of moon snails makes them unlikely to be mistaken for any other snail. Likewise, the emptied shells of their prey bear drill holes that are characteristic: typically located near the hinge, and neatly countersunk. The mark is unique—and you can deduce that the predation resulted in a full moon snail.

Razor Clam

Latin name: *Siliqua patula*

Description: Narrow, elongated shell up to 6½ inches long, 2½ inches wide; shiny olive green to brown; two white siphons fused except at the tips.

Habitat: Coastal shorelines, in open, broadly sloping sandy beaches with strong surf; in the lowest part exposed by tides; also just offshore and to depths of 180 feet; not found in Puget Sound.

If you had to choose a shell for a soft-bodied animal living on a surf-pounded beach, you would probably select one that was thick, and possibly compact. Natural selection doesn't always end up with the most obvious solution, however. The razor clam is encased in a thin, brittle shell, yet it lives only on wide-open, wave-hammered sandy beaches.

This apparent design flaw is compensated for by the clam's digging ability. Many clams can burrow, but their best efforts can't match the racing razor clam: it has been clocked traveling an inch a second. Some clam diggers suggest that a beginner who misses a razor clam on the first or second scoop should look for another one rather than trying to out-dig the thing. In order to survive on the wave-washed beach, these clams are especially sensitive to movement and pressure, so experienced clammers depend on the element of surprise to capture their prey.

The slenderness of its shell helps the razor clam dig so quickly. An escaping animal extends its pointed foot as far as possible down into the sand. The tip of the foot then swells as blood is rapidly pumped into it. Now anchored in the sand, the muscular foot contracts, pulling the rest of the body downward. Because the razor clam's foot is wider in diameter than the streamlined shell, the shell follows swiftly through the tunnel created for it. Additionally, the front end of the animal expels water around the foot, "softening" the sand ahead to further facilitate burrowing.

But unless it is in danger, the razor clam is usually found near the surface, feeding on tiny organisms, particularly diatoms (one-celled microscopic algae), found in the waves. Using its siphon, the clam sucks in water for oxygen and nutrition, and its gills filter out the food particles.

The shape of its shell earned the clam its common name: it resembles an old-fashioned straight razor folded into its slender case. Another creature, named for its resemblance to a vegetable, often lives inside the clam's shell. Like its host, the little pea crab is a filter feeder. The pea crab has been considered a commensal, meaning that although it lives inside the shell of the clam, it doesn't harm it. However, some biologists suspect that the crab, which lodges in the clam's gill cavity, may slow the clam's growth—making it a parasite instead of a commensal. The accommodating razor clam also often hosts a species of worm that is considered a commensal. It attaches itself with a sucker disk near the clam's siphon and, like the pea crab, selects tidbits from the incoming siphoned water.

All three creatures survive quite well within that relatively fragile shell, despite the inherent danger of living on the beach where the waves land hardest. The razor clam is never found in protected bays and estuaries—it demands the tumbling, oxygen-rich waves of the open shore. And it has been naturally selected to live there—not by having a sensible thick shell, but by being phenomenally fleet of foot.

Beach Hopper

Latin name: *Megalorchestia californiana*

Description: About ½ inch long; brownish white, grayish white, or ivory body; antennae as long as or longer than body and bright orange; seven pairs of legs.

Habitat: On sandy ocean beaches, buried along high-tide line or on washed-up kelp and other seaweed.

In her 1955 classic *The Edge of the Sea,* Rachel Carson writes that the tiny and seemingly insignificant beach hopper portrays "one of those dramatic moments of evolution, in which a creature abandons an old way of life for a new." She suggests that the beach hopper's ancestors lived in the ocean and that in the distant future its descendants will likely be terrestrial.

But, for now, the beach hopper can live neither too far from the water nor too close to it. The tiny critters still have gills, located on their leg joints, and require moisture to breathe. But many species are poor swimmers and can drown if submerged too long. So they live on the margin, navigating the area between dry sand and lapping tide.

These little creatures are not insects, as might reasonably be supposed. They are crustaceans, relatives of the pillbugs and sowbugs found in backyards and woodpiles, which are a little ahead of the beach hopper on the evolutionary transition to landlubbers.

Beach hopper, beach flea, sand hopper, sand flea—all these names refer to the same type of animal. More confusing than picking a common name is the attempt to identify individuals by specific scientific names—there are many species of beach hoppers, and they can look bafflingly similar, even under magnification. However, *Megalorchestia californiana* is one of the most common species found on Northwest shores.

M. californiana prefers open beaches and tends to congregate on washed-up masses of seaweed. If you lift up a pile of kelp, sometimes hundreds of beach hoppers will explode from their refuge, leaping wildly about until they land back on the seaweed or bury themselves safely in the sand. These particular hoppers can be identified by their long orange or pinkish antennae. (Another common species, *Traskorchestia traskiana*, is found on sheltered beaches or bays and has bluish legs.)

If they're not nestled in seaweed, beach hoppers pass the day above the high-tide line, buried headfirst in the sand, and emerge at dusk to feed. The hoppers are scavengers that eat what the tide tosses up, especially seaweed. At night, impressive armies of the leaping little crustaceans storm the beaches, discovering and devouring what the tide has left them.

While foraging, they must watch out for their enemies, especially the inch-long rove beetles that also emerge for nocturnal feeding. Beach hoppers escape their predators with prodigious jumps. (It's this ability alone that earns them comparison to fleas—hoppers don't bite people.) They use their back two pairs of legs for jumping and are propelled by a sudden snap of the abdomen.

The females hold their fertilized eggs in special brood pouches on their legs and carry the young everywhere until they are hatched. Then, at night, they are released onto the sand, miniature versions of their parents that immediately take up the rhythm and routine of feeding and burrowing.

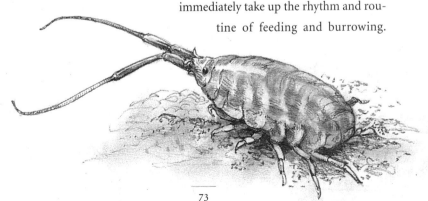

Before dawn, the hoppers make their way back up the beach to dig their dens, reportedly orienting themselves by the moon.

By daylight or high tide, the little beachcombers' work is finished and they are sealed away until the return of darkness and a lowering tide. You can look for the small round holes near the high-tide line, which are their previous night's burrows. (Occupied dens are closed off with sand granules, so you're not likely to see them.)

Beach hoppers avoid the waves yet are still bound to the ocean. Although their gilled legs are tiny, beach hoppers straddle the wide transition zone between salt water and dry land.

Geoduck

Latin name: *Panopea abrupta* (formerly *generosa*)

Description: Grayish white shell grows to 8 inches long, with irregular concentric rings; siphon can extend to about 39 inches.

Habitat: From several hundred feet offshore up to the low-tide line; also in bays and estuaries. Prefers sand or mud, but can be found in gravel; typically burrowed 2 to 3 feet down.

By student vote, the geoduck narrowly defeated the banana slug to become the mascot of The Evergreen State College in Olympia, Washington, where I studied marine biology. The rather outrageous clam seems a fitting representative for the rather unorthodox college.

Geoducks (pronounced "gooey-ducks") are outrageous by virtue of size alone. They are the world's largest burrowing clam—giants can weigh ten pounds. More often the adults weigh in at two pounds, but lucky diggers sometimes unearth beefy 'ducks weighing six or seven pounds—as much as a newborn baby.

Their shells are a rounded rectangular shape, partially covered with a thin, brownish "skin" that protects against sand abrasion. Although the shells often grow to seven or eight inches long, they are not nearly large enough to contain the paunchy animals. The geoducks' bodies bulge out of their gaping shells (hence Evergreen's motto: *Omnia exteris,* or "Let it all hang out"). They get away with this obvious flaw in their armor only by being so deeply buried that few predators can reach them.

Various bottom-dwelling fish might nip off siphon tips poking out of the seabed, but the geoduck's most cunning predators are people. Commercial divers, using high-pressure hoses, can blast the animals loose from their homes at the rate of two or three per minute. Clam diggers on the beach, however, must be knowledgeable, persistent, and properly equipped to reach one of these trophies. When its siphon blasts a load of cold seawater and disappears beneath the sand, a 'duck might appear to be digging. But adult geoducks do not dig at all. The well-endowed geoduck simply contracts—and contracts, and contracts—that extravagant siphon as far as it can. Only a digger's most dogged determination will eventually reveal the meaty bivalve waiting at the bottom of up to four feet of densely packed sand and mud.

Given that, the creature's original name of *gweduc*, bestowed by the Nisqually people, is entirely logical. Before it was corrupted into nonsensical English, this favored clam was named "dig deep." Still, the ludicrous name is part of the oversized animal's charm.

Geoducks make more 'ducks without ever having to leave their deep, cozy burrows or even meet a member of the opposite sex. They simply release either eggs or sperm from their siphons and allow the current to make introductions. It's been estimated that one female geoduck produces up to fifty million eggs per year. The relatively few lucky fertilized eggs develop into swimming larvae, which metamorphose into miniature adults.

These young geoducks burrow into the substrate, digging deeper as their siphons grow longer. If they survive to the end of their second year, they are probably deep enough to be safe from most predators. As they mature and grow heavier, the size of their foot does not keep pace, and eventually the animals are as deep down as they are ever going to get. The geoducks settle in, inhaling oxygen and plankton through their snorkel-like siphons, and exhaling waste as well as sperm or eggs. These outlandish animals live for one hundred and forty years—or perhaps more. Unless, of course, they are unearthed by someone intending to savor the sublime taste of my alma mater's mascot.

Sandpipers

Latin name: *Calidris* spp.

Description: From 4³/₄ inches to 7 inches, depending on species; different species of sandpipers share these characteristics: slender bills; winter and summer plumages differ, but colors include grays, browns, and whites and may be streaked or mottled.

Habitat: Annual visitors to Pacific Northwest sand or gravel beaches, coastal mudflats, flooded fields, marshes. Migration generally peaks mid-April to mid-May.

I f you regularly walk on sandy beaches, you have already made acquaintance with little birds called sandpipers that do the same. Instead of traveling the length of the beach, however, these shorebirds tend to move up and down the slope of it, following the tides— and the food. They're not out for a casual stroll; the sandpipers are loading up on calories during one of their stops on a marathon migration.

Sandpipers can be a bewildering lot. There are many different kinds, and they wear different feathers

Dunlin

Sanderling

Least Sandpiper

depending on the time of year and whether they are juveniles or adults. The group contains not only birds that are *called* sandpipers, like the western and least sandpipers (*C. mauri* and *C. minutilla*), but also birds like dunlins and sanderlings (*C. alpina* and *C. alba*). An astute observer can sometimes distinguish the birds by niceties including leg color, slight curving of bills, and an inch more or less in body length. But when sandpipers are running, flying, or a bit too far away for details, it's hard to say who's who. Which is probably why birders coined the generic (and energetic) term "peep" to mean any small *Calidris* species.

The peeps sort themselves out when feeding according to slight differences in the length of their bills. Sanderlings scurry ahead of and chase after lapping waves as if they don't want to get their feet wet. They nab newly deposited or newly revealed prey off the sand or from just below the surface. The western sandpiper also goes after surface food but is willing to wade right into the water, sometimes submerging its head to feed. Dunlins are more likely to probe deeper into the sand or mud. And the tiny least sandpipers prefer foraging at the high-tide line. All these birds feed on marine invertebrates such as beach hoppers, tiny shrimp, and insects. Their differentiation in feeding strategies explains how so many similar birds can feed on the same kinds of prey without being in competition.

Marine invertebrates are offered in bulk on the Pacific Coast, and the sandpipers stop here on their transcontinental travels to load up. (Many overwinter too.) In spring the birds are all adults and sport their breeding plumage, so they are usually easier to identify. The migration time is relatively brief, but huge numbers of birds stop over in Washington and Oregon on their way from South or Central America to their Arctic nesting areas.

They fly these long distances to take advantage of insect hatches and relatively few predatory mammals on the tundra of Siberia and northern Alaska. Many sandpipers lay four eggs, which are brooded by both parents. In some cases the family remains together until the young are ready to fly. In others, like the dunlins and least sandpipers, the females leave the young in the care of the father long before they fledge.

Upon the shorebirds' return to the Northwest from June onward, some are still in breeding plumage, while others have assumed their duller non-breeding feathers. Juveniles also show up to further confuse matters. Dunlins generally don't return until late October, but they tend to stick around and are the Pacific Northwest's most common overwintering shorebird, roosting on sandy beaches throughout the winter, biding their time until low tide. During this season, you can safely assume that any large flying, flashing flocks you see are dunlins.

Sandpipers attempting to elude predators take to the air in stunning synchronized displays. A merlin or peregrine falcon will try to zero in on one single bird, so the birds' best defense is to remain solidly together as they elude capture. The flock wheels and dives, rises, spreads apart or pulls back together. Their plumage appears to blink white and dark as the birds turn their bodies from front to back. Slow-motion studies have revealed what our eyes cannot detect: rather than all the birds turning at the exact same time, the edge of the flock leads the way. Each following bird catches "the wave" in turn, quickly enough that the action appears simultaneous. Using this choreographed flight, the sandpipers manage to confound some of their predators as readily as they do many of the birders who try to identify them.

Western and Glaucous-Winged Gulls

Latin names: *Larus glaucescens* (glaucous-winged); *L. occidentalis* (western)

Description: About 26 inches; white head, neck, and breast; gray wings and back (breeding plumage); yellow beak with red spot near tip on lower half; pink legs.

Habitat: Along coast, in estuaries and bays, also garbage dumps and sewage treatment plants.

Slipped smoothly into conversation, the statement "There's no such bird as a seagull" would probably win a lot of barroom bets. Open any bird book and you'll find it's true. Although plenty of gulls live by the sea, they go by names such as herring gull, ring-billed gull, and California gull. Thirteen different species regularly visit the Pacific Northwest, and there's not a single "seagull" among them.

Of those thirteen, the two most commonly seen along the coast are the western gull and the glaucous-winged gull. They're both relatively large gulls with pink legs, and the best way to tell them apart is by the color of their backs; the western is the darker of the two. Glaucous-winged are named for their color ("glaucous" meaning a frosty gray). These two species are most numerous because they both breed along the Pacific Northwest coast. Glaucous-winged tend to nest in Washington and farther north, westerns in Oregon and south. But the two intermingle and sometimes interbreed, creating offspring that look a bit like each of them (and, coincidentally, also like Thayer's gulls). These hybrids are so common they're sometimes given their own unofficial name of "Puget Sound gull."

Identifying gulls is not for the faint of heart. Different species can look maddeningly similar, but serious birders look for subtle clues: the color contrast between the back and the wing tips, and the leg and bill colors. Further complicating matters, each species has different breeding and nonbreeding (winter) plumages, and their juveniles are a variety of browns in their first years, shading into grays and whites as they age. (It may help somewhat to know that the ring-billed and California species are the most common inland gulls.)

The two species that claim the coast breed in large colonies on outer islands and rocky cliffs. Gull couples form long-term, perhaps lifelong, relationships, returning annually to the same territory and sometimes even to the same nest. Their three eggs are held in a bulky cup of grasses, seaweeds, and feathers. Parents take turns incubating the eggs and standing guard. They defend their territorial borders fiercely, and even seize and eat neighboring chicks that stray from their own nests. Glaucous-winged gulls are especially prone to cannibalizing other birds' chicks and are a major cause of mortality in those younger than three weeks.

Both parents feed the chicks, who elicit a regurgitation response by pecking at the red spot on the lower half of the parent's bill. The young are programmed to zero in on this target: they'll peck with equal insistence at a stick with a similar spot painted on it, even though the stick looks nothing like a bill and is not attached to anything that looks like a bird.

Once the young have fledged, they learn all the gull tricks, such as swaggering up to picnickers to beg handouts and breaking open mussels and clams by dropping them from the air onto rocks. They learn the locations of canneries and other hot eating spots, and that following clammers on the beach and fishing boats at sea often reaps rewards.

Primarily scavengers, gulls have long been lauded for their efforts in helping to clean beaches of carcasses and garbage. They also pirate morsels from other birds, and they manage to choke down such huge food items—such as sea stars—that it almost makes you gag to watch them. Gulls are so very good at eating nearly anything that they can be found in many places other than the sea. As my husband Tim likes to say, if there are seagulls, then there must also be reservoir gulls, dump gulls, and supermarket-parking-lot gulls. You can bet on it.

Mole Crab

Latin name: *Emerita analoga*

Description: About 2 inches long; egg-shaped body, grayish above and whitish underneath; ten legs that tuck compactly in against the body, no claws; eyes on tiny stalks.

Habitat: Buried just beneath the surface of wave-swept, sandy ocean beaches.

My sister-in-law and I were leaving the beach when a little V-shaped ripple in the sand caught her eye. Digging her fingers in a few inches behind the indentation, Anne unearthed a curious little creature that neither of us could identify. It's apparently possible to take lots of walks on sandy beaches without ever noticing the mole crabs buried just underfoot.

Various fishes and shorebirds know the mole crabs are there, and feast on them, and people who fish often use them as bait. But the ovoid creature, nearly two inches long, was new to Anne and me—and we hadn't a clue what in that expanse of sand it could find to eat or even which end of it was the front or rear. Before Anne reburied it, the little armored beast scuttled suddenly across the sand, and we figured we at least knew the forwardmost end was the head. We were wrong.

My seashore field guides later explained that the mole crab, or sand crab, always travels backward, whether it is swimming or digging—or crawling, like ours, although they rarely crawl because they are rarely on the surface of the beach. During low tide they remain buried in sand, facing the ocean. When the waves return, the mole crabs at the lower end of the beach catch a ride, jockeying their way to positions higher up in the swash zone and quickly reburying themselves. Only the animal's eyestalks and a small pair of antennae, which come together to form a breathing tube, protrude from the sand. As the wave recedes, the crabs unfurl two long feathery antennae. Detritus—tiny bits of plants and animals—become entangled in these plumes. The antennae are drawn into the mouthparts and combed of detritus, and uncoiled again as the food is swallowed. The process continues with each wave until ebb tide, when the mole crabs often ride their way back down the shore, burying themselves again closer to the ocean. The V-shaped indentation that Anne noticed is caused by the deflection of water from around the antennae and eyestalks of the crab. It's also possible to find them by looking for tiny escaping air bubbles.

These little crustaceans usually live in dense clusters, with the females, who are larger, buried closer to the ocean than the males. However, during the mating season males are strongly attracted to females who are ready to lay eggs. If such a female buries herself in the sand, nearby males will scuttle out to rebury themselves near her. The males also sometimes attach themselves to the females by means of a suction disk on each of two of their back legs. The larger female may carry two or three of these tag-along males up and down the beach with her as she follows the tide. About twelve hours before she lays her eggs, one or more of the hitchhikers deposit mucus ribbons laden with sperm on the underside of her body. The female will carry the fertilized eggs for many weeks as they develop, changing from

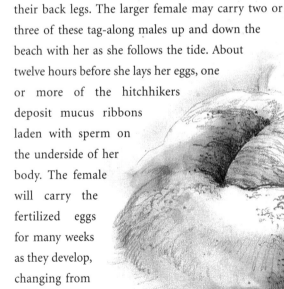

orange to gray. The larvae are eventually released into the waves and spend the next four months or more traveling the ocean. The young initially look nothing at all like their parents, but through successive molts they eventually resemble miniature adults.

The offspring can settle as far north as Alaska, but in colder waters they are unable to reproduce. Likewise, the colonies north of the Oregon-California border occasionally die out, and it may be years before another swarm of larvae arrives from warmer waters to repopulate a given beach.

But if the tide and your timing are right, you can watch for tell-tale V ripples the next time you walk along a sandy beach, and carefully unearth a mole crab. And when it reburies itself or scuttles backward across the sand, you'll be able to identify (accurately) which end is the head.

Limpets

Latin name: Class Gastropoda; various genera and species

Description: Most from 1 to 3 inches, but length varies according to species; soft-bodied, two-tentacled animal encased in hard, broadly cone-shaped shell; keyhole limpets have a small hole in the top of shell.

Habitat: Differs according to species, including surf-pounded rocks, eelgrass or surfgrass, shells of other snails, vertical surfaces, crevices, or rocky upper reaches of high tide.

Try to pluck a limpet off a rock and you'll discover this mollusk's main defense strategy: suction. A limpet adheres so tightly to rocks that you could end up breaking its shell before it would loosen its grip. Staying attached to its substrate is important to a creature that has a soft and vulnerable body tucked into a single shell. Bivalves like mussels and scallops can clamp their two shells tightly shut; snails can seal their single shell with a hard door called an operculum; but limpets, like chitons and abalones, rely on suction power to protect them from pounding surf and potential predators.

Many limpets can sense and respond to the approach or touch of a sea star. As the hunter nears, the limpet hikes up its shell like a Southern belle raising her hoop skirt, and glides off in another direction. This is called the "running" escape defense, apparently named by a researcher with a sense of humor. Still, this member of the snail family need not be much of a sprinter to outdistance a creeping sea star. Other limpets respond to the predator's approach by simply letting go of their rock and tumbling to a (hopefully) safer location.

The rough keyhole limpet (*Diodora aspera*) has another option. This common limpet of Puget Sound and the open coast also lifts its striped skirt at the approach of a sea star, but instead of running, it extends fleshy curtains down over the foot and up over the shell. The common sea star is usually deterred by this defense, perhaps because its tube feet cannot grip the slippery surface. But a disagreeable chemical "taste" may be the real deterrent. Other sea stars are known to prey on the rough keyhole limpet, regardless. But this creature usually has a hidden cohort who springs into action when its host is under attack. Almost every rough keyhole limpet carries a worm, *Arctonoe vittata,* coiled underneath its shell. In this symbiotic you-help-me-and-I'll-help-you relationship, the worm receives protection and access to food. It pays its rent by helping to ward off attacking sea stars, reportedly biting their tube feet and hastening their retreat.

Most limpets are vegetarians who wait until the tide covers them—especially the night tide—to creep about in search of algae. They extend their two sensory tentacles and begin foraging. The barest film of new algae feeds a limpet, and it eats by rasping a file-like tongue called a radula over the rocks, both breaking up food particles and conveying them to the mouth. Many limpets cruise a specific home territory, bulldozing or otherwise uprooting potential homesteaders such as barnacle spawn. Some species have a very specific resting spot to which they return with the falling tide. An individual uses the same spot throughout its life, and over time its shell carves an exact outline into the rock. The returning limpet aligns itself precisely in its "home scar" and settles down. As the tide recedes, the animal retains some water, which allows it to breathe until the next tide.

Most limpets also rely on the tides to mix their sperm and eggs. The sexes are separate (although in some species all young limpets are male, becoming female as they mature), and each looses its eggs or sperm to meet in the water. The resulting larvae swim about for a time as they develop, eventually finding habitats that match their particular species requirements.

The dunce cap, or whitecap limpet (*Acmaea mitra*) prefers rocks that harbor an encrusting pink coralline algae. This knobby pink stuff is the dunce cap's food, but it often finds a hold on the creature's shell and grows there as well, covering and camouflaging the animal. (This helps not only the limpet, but also the lucky algae riding safely on its predator's back.) You'll often find the dunce cap limpet's empty tall, conical, one-inch shell on the beach.

The digit or ribbed limpet (*Lottia digitalis* [formerly *Collisella digitalis*]) prefers vertical rock faces that receive some wave action. Other limpets attach to strands of eelgrass, surfgrass, or kelp, or the shells of black turban snails. Limpets can be found in specific niches from high-tide rocks to grasses, and all have a solid grip on the place where they live.

Common Sea Star

Latin name: *Pisaster ochraceus*

Description: 8 to 10 inches in diameter; usually orange or purple (though it can be yellow or brown); a network of small, white spines shows up against the darker background color; five arms.

Habitat: Rocky tide pools and below the low-tide line.

It's the star of the tide pool: *Pisaster ochraceus,* a.k.a. the common, purple, or ochre sea star. It is the creature everyone can identify, the one we most hope to see. This animal is commonly called a "starfish," but scientists and naturalists prefer the term "sea star" because it is clearly not a fish. It's an echinoderm—a spiny-skinned animal that can be divided into five equal parts. A sea star is more closely related to sea urchins and sand dollars than to fish.

Having neither head nor tail, the sea star moves in any direction that one of its arms points and can reverse direction without turning around. It's true that a sea star can regenerate a lost arm—or two or three; the central disk alone can regenerate all of the arms.

Male and female sea stars look identical, but even the creatures themselves have no real need to differentiate. With the arrival of springtime and warmer water temperatures, the males simply release sperm and the females release eggs to mix in the ocean currents. The fertilized eggs become swimming larvae, which eventually settle on the ocean floor and grow into proper sea stars.

If you look closely at the upper surface of an adult sea star, you'll notice a small round opening—the anus—near the center of the animal. You're less likely to notice the very tiny pincers called *pedicellariae* that cover the animal's entire upper surface. But if you rest a hairy hand or arm briefly against the star, you may feel the tug of these tiny pincers when you pull away. The pedicellariae keep the animal clean by crushing any minute larvae or parasites that happen to land on it.

The star's mouth is located in the center of its underside. When it finds a delectable meal, perhaps a snail or a small crab, the star extrudes its stomach outside its body through its mouth. The stomach looks something like a little plastic bag as it envelops the prey. Juices secreted by the stomach walls dissolve the smaller animal's flesh, and the star absorbs the resulting liquid.

The everted stomach is able to slide into incredibly thin cracks, which is useful when the star pries apart the shell of its favorite food, the mussel. The common sea star's penchant for California mussels gives it a pivotal role along the rocky coast. When scientists removed all the common sea stars from a tidal community, they found that it was soon overgrown with mussels—which eventually crowded out all other species. Thanks to its appetite, the sea star is in large part responsible for the variety of life found along rocky seashores.

Lining the undersides of the star's arms are many slender but amazingly strong tube feet tipped with suction cups. The tube feet use hydraulic pressure to adhere to a mussel's shell and to hold the star in place on rocks in pounding surf. The small feet also enable the animal to travel: a sea star can move at a rate of three inches per minute by reaching out with its tube feet, planting the suckers, and pulling its body along.

The ends of the sea star's arms contain the animal's sensory abilities. Tube feet there have no suction disks but are able to feel and smell, and an eyespot is located at the very tip of each arm. Although the eyespots don't allow vision, they are believed to be sensitive to light.

Ochre star, purple star, or common star. Starfish or sea star. Whatever name you prefer, it's not only one of the most common animals you'll find on the rocky Pacific Coast; it's also one of the most influential.

Sea Urchins

Latin name: *Strongylocentrotus* spp.

Description: From 3 inches to 12 inches in diameter, depending on species; spine-covered, ball-shaped or slightly flattened animals; purple, red, or green, depending on species.

Habitat: Coastal shorelines, from exposed, wave-pounded rocks to quiet shores; different species prefer different habitats.

ea urchins, with their rounded bodies and stiffly moving spines, are more often compared to pincushions than to other animals. Even their closest relatives, sea stars and sand dollars, don't look much like them, though they share certain characteristics.

All three types of animals have many tube feet—slender appendages used for locomotion, respiration, and grabbing any food tidbits that float by. In sea urchins, the tube feet protrude randomly among the spines, over the entire body of the animal. The three cousins also have similar five-jawed chewing mechanisms used for eating, and all three have tiny, jawed pedicellariae on stalks, which are used for defense and to keep the animals clean. The pedicellariae are scattered across the sea urchins' bodies, like their tube feet. The three jaws of each pedicellaria grasp and remove the larvae of barnacles and mussels that are looking for a place they can call home. The biting pedicellariae also defend the urchin against attack from predators like sea stars. Both tube feet and pedicellariae can be regrown if they are detached.

The three relatives all have five-part radial symmetry, meaning that their internal structures are arranged around the central point of their mouths and the animal could be divided into five equal parts. This symmetry is

sea urchin mouth—
located on animal's underside

more
obvious in
five-armed sea
stars and in the five-
petaled design on the tops of
sand dollars than in the many-spined
sea urchin.

Those spines—which can point toward an enemy or away from it, so that the pedicellariae can better rise to the attack—also get the sea urchin from one place to another. The urchin uses the spines to "walk" as if it were tippy-toeing or stilt-walking.

The Northwest's three common urchins are sensibly named according to their coloration. The green sea urchin (*S. droebachiensis*) grows to about three inches across and is usually found in calm waters from Washington northward. When the purple sea urchin (*S. purpuratus*) is young, it could be mistaken for a green urchin except that its habitat choice can give it away. Purple urchins are almost never found in quiet tide pools. Preferring strong wave action, they actually burrow into rock to help them hold on. The purples accomplish this by rasping their spines against the rock, and perhaps by using their sharp-tipped jaws as well. Because they begin this process when they are small, the opening of the resulting hole is smaller in diameter than the animal that made it. As the urchin grows, it can carve itself into a hole that it can't get out of after reaching its full size of up to four inches in diameter. The surrounding rock protects the animal, and the never-ending waves deliver its food.

The red sea urchin (*S. franciscanus*) can be found in both quiet and wilder waters, and may grow to a foot in diameter. Its spines are longer than those of either the green or the purple urchin.

Male and female urchins release their sperm or eggs simultaneously. Females reportedly produce twenty million eggs in one season. The small swimming creatures that develop from the fertilized eggs are bilaterally symmetrical, but eventually they settle in an appropriate place and metamorphose into the radial symmetry of the adults.

An urchin's mouth is located in the center of its underside; its anus is in the center of its top side. The animals eat algae, seaweed, and plankton. In turn, they are eaten by some sea stars, seagulls, and people who consider urchin gonads a delicacy.

These little bundles of spines are some of the most common creatures found along Northwest shorelines. You'll find different sea urchin species on wave-swept ocean rocks than you'll discover in Puget Sound tide pools, but both places boast plenty of the small, spiky beach balls.

Blue and California Mussels

Latin names: *Mytilus trossulus* (blue mussel); *M. californianus* (California mussel)

Description: Blue mussels to 4 inches long; California mussels to more than 10 inches. Blue and black shells are a rounded, elongated triangular shape.

Habitat: Blue mussels: tide pools, quieter waters inland and on coast, also associated with California mussels in wave-swept area. California mussels: wave-swept rocks on coast.

A mussel larva looking for a place to settle embodies the real estate agent's maxim: the three most important considerations are location, location, and location. If the young mussel lands too high on a rock, it will die of dehydration and exposure; too low on the rock and it enters the territory most frequented by its archenemy, the sea star. Perhaps this difficulty in choosing just the right spot is the reason that the larvae are predisposed to attach themselves to already established mussels. By simply having stayed alive, the elders prove their location is a good one. But even this option has its own inherent danger. Too many mussels attaching to other mussels that are attached to the relatively few who are actually anchored to a rock can pull the whole shebang into the ocean.

But that, of course, would open up a nice patch of prime real estate for the next infant mussel that swims along. During their young and wayfaring stage, larvae are nothing like the adults. They live and feed in surface waters and are dispersed with the currents. Eventually they settle on a substrate and change into their adult form—but they can be quite choosy about where they will live and can delay maturity to continue rambling until they find the site that suits them.

Even after they are established, blue mussels (also called bay mussels and occasionally edible or foolish mussels) have a limited ability to move. Mussels fasten themselves to rocks, pilings, and other mussels by byssal threads, collectively called a byssus ("BISS-us"). These tough elastic threads, produced by the animal's byssal gland, are made of protein, like hair. By touching the gland with its foot, the mussel draws a thread to the substrate, where it attaches. This action is repeated many times until threads radiate outward around the animal like many guy wires steadying a pole. The byssus changes color from brown to white and hardens in the water. Even after the byssus hardens, a blue mussel can move a small distance by throwing threads in the direction it wants to go and then using muscle contraction to slide forward.

Mussels live clumped together, tightly nestled in large beds that may cover several square feet. Blue mussels occasionally live on exposed rocks pummeled by the ocean but are more likely to be found in quiet tide pools, estuaries, and bays. They grow to about three inches in length and have smooth shells outlined with irregular concentric rings. California mussels are the species more likely to be found in areas of heavy surf and wave action. They have stronger byssal threads to anchor them and grow larger than the blue mussel—usually to five inches, but sometimes reaching ten inches or more. Their shells also have concentric rings, but these are rippled instead of smooth.

Mussels feed when the tide covers them, and their shells gape open like the mouths of hungry baby birds. The animals siphon in the water, pulling it over their gills, which have the dual responsibility of breathing and food-gathering. The gills simultaneously extract dissolved oxygen from the water and filter the tiny plankton that mussels eat. (During the summer months mussels, like clams, sometimes ingest a microscopic organism responsible for "red tides," which has a toxin that builds up in the creature's gut. This toxin has been known to paralyze or kill people who eat filter feeders such as mussels. It is imperative to heed posted notices warning of shellfish poisoning.)

The sexes are separate in mussels, and their sperm and eggs unite in the water to create swimming larvae. Relatively few of these survive their rambling adolescence. Each young mussel that does escape predation eventually settles down, finds itself a nice home, and puts down some byssus threads.

Anemones

Latin name: *Anthopleura* spp.

Description: 1 inch to 12 inches in diameter, depending on species; disk fringed with tentacles is attached to substrate by a fleshy column. When tentacles are pulled in at low tide, anemones look like nondescript blobs.

Habitat: Tide pools, surge channels, rock faces, also underwater offshore.

Anemones are often described as animals that look like plants. Their circular disks surrounded by petal-like tentacles do resemble exotic hothouse flowers. But make no mistake: the pretty anemone is a carnivore, and it kills its prey with harpoonlike weapons.

The giant green anemone (*Anthopleura xanthogrammica*) grows ten to twelve inches in diameter and is a lovely shade of new-spring green. Its coloration is due both to its own pigmentation and to a large population of one-celled algae that live inside it in a mutually beneficial relationship. In exchange for protection, a place to live, and nutrients from the waste of their host, the algae photosynthesize and produce carbohydrates used by both themselves and the anemone.

Like all anemones, the giant green has stinging cells called nematocysts, which are especially concentrated in the tentacles. These cells fire harpoonlike microscopic threads and discharge a toxin into predator or prey—or into your finger, should you touch a tentacle. (The relative thickness of our skin prevents us from feeling anything but an interesting sticky sensation, although a very few people might have an allergic reaction to the toxin.) As the tentacle gently cleaves to your finger, its harpoons fire, but there's no difficulty pulling it away when you're finished playing Moby Dick. It's a different story, and a different ending, for prey like mussels and small crabs or fish. Once paralyzed by the nematocysts, they are drawn into the anemone's mouth (the bellybutton-looking protuberance in the center of the animal) and swallowed whole. The anemone's powerful digestive juices then dissolve the flesh of the unfortunate prey, and its undigestible bits, like shell fragments, are spit back out.

More numerous than the giant green is an anemone that seems to have no widely agreed on common name. *A. elegantissima* is sometimes called either the "elegant" or the "aggregating" anemone. This indecision almost seems appropriate, since the animal itself comes in two forms, one solitary and one that lives in colonies. The solitary form grows to eight inches in diameter and resembles a giant green anemone, except for the straight, dark lines radiating from mouth to tentacles. In the aggregating form, more commonly seen, the disk diameter varies from about one to three inches and the tentacles are often tipped a delicate pink or lavender.

Like the giant green anemone, an individual A. *elegantissima* is either male or female and produces either sperm or eggs. These are released via the mouth and mix in the current to produce swimming larvae. But an A. *elegantissima* who finds itself alone on a bare rock has a second reproductive option: cloning. After pulling itself in opposite directions for about two days, the animal tears in half. This is a particularly fast way to fill an open space, and the anemone goes on producing exact replicas of itself (same gender, same coloration) until it runs out of room—or meets up with another A. *elegantissima* colony that has been busily cloning *it*self.

Such a meeting does not go well. After repeated jostling, war erupts between the two colonies. The anemones on the outskirts of each group prepare for battle. Special structures called *acrorhagi*, located on the upper portion of the anemone's column and loaded with nematocysts, begin to swell. In what looks to us like slow motion, a combatant rears up and clouts an enemy with its knoblike acrorhagi. The attacked anemone may choose to stand its ground and fight back, but usually it contracts as if cringing and gradually shuffles away. But there is only so far an anemone can retreat with its crowded clone family behind it. Eventually the colonies, after attack and counterattack, form a no-anemones land. This is a clearly visible strip between the two communities that was once assumed to be a pathway for snails and limpets.

Characteristics such as these demilitarized zones and the weapon-wielding tentacles reveal that, despite appearances, the pretty anemone is really an animal. It may look like a demure plant, but an anemone is no shrinking violet.

Purple Shore Crab

Latin name: *Hemigrapsus nudus*

Description: Shell of back up to 2 inches wide; predominantly purple-tinged, but may be reddish brown or green; purple-red spots on claws.

Habitat: Under rocks or scurrying around the upper tidal area; rocky beaches and some estuaries; occasionally ventures onto sandy beach, if nearby.

The right way to pick up a little purple shore crab, should you wish to do so, is to nab it quickly and firmly from behind, catching it between thumb and forefinger. The wrong way to pick up a crab is by a claw clamped onto your finger. I've done it both ways and the first is definitely preferable.

Purple shore crabs are the crabs most often encountered by ocean beachcombers and tide-pool enthusiasts. These crustaceans can spend long periods of time without direct contact with seawater, so they are often found in the higher levels of tide pools. If you don't see any scuttling around, you can often find them by lifting loose rocks (be sure to replace the rocks just as you found them). Purple shore crabs measure at best a mere two inches across their backs, and when they wave their little claws at you menacingly, its a bit like a belligerent tot hollering, "Try it—go on, I dare ya!"

But should your fingers slip when you make your move to pick up the tyke, you'll find its claws surprisingly strong. It seems ridiculous that such a little thing can cause as much pain as it does, but you don't usually laugh about it until the beast has been pried off.

If you grab it the right way, however, you'll have a chance to look it over in detail; the reddish purple spots on its claws that identify it, the individual coloration, which might range from brownish red through green and purple with white splotches thrown in. The carapace (back) is shaped like a rounded rectangle, with three jagged "teeth" on the front margin.

While you've got it in hand, note the lack of hairs on its legs—this is what gives it the species name *nudus* and distinguishes it from the similar green crab. The green or mud crab (*H. oregonensis*) is usually found in mud flats, but the two crab territories overlap in gravelly, muddy areas. (In addition to its hairy legs, the green crab is usually grayish green and lacks its relation's purplish dots on the claws.) The crab's first pair of legs end, of course, in its waving pincers, and each of the other eight legs ends in a pointy hook that helps the animal get a grip on slippery rocks.

Purple shore crabs feed mostly on seaweed and other algae but also scavenge any dead animals they may come across. They are in turn eaten mostly by shorebirds and some fish. Crabs are especially vulnerable to predation when molting, which they must do throughout their lifetimes in order to grow.

Female crabs carry their eggs behind a broad flap on their undersides. The spongy egg mass is so large that it pushes the flap open and bulges out the gap. The eggs eventually hatch as larvae into the ocean. These tiny, transparent, fanciful-looking, big-eyed creatures are so unlike their parents that they were originally described as a separate species. But after a succession of molts, each looks like a miniature adult, complete with menacing little claws. Its combative spirit might really grab you.

Chitons

Latin names:*Katharina tunicata; Cryptochiton stelleri; Mopalia muscosa*

Description: From 1½ inches to 14 inches long, depending on species; oval or oblong; upper surface hard, eight valves may be visible; lower surface mostly a large fleshy foot, unseen unless the creature is pried off its rock.

Habitat: Tide pools, shallow waters, and below low-tide line on rocky shores.

Chitons like the West best. They are bigger and more abundant here, and there are more species along the Pacific Coast than on the Atlantic Coast—or just about anywhere else in the world. Chitons (pronounced "KI-tens") are marine snails characterized by the eight plates or "valves" that make up their shell. (The "butterfly shells" found by beachcombers are actually the valves of dead chitons.) Hard flesh called a girdle surrounds the valves and covers them to a greater or lesser extent, depending on species. This is all that is usually seen of the mollusk: it has no tentacles to extend and is often clamped so tightly to a rock it can't easily be dislodged. Its overlapping valves allow it to conform neatly to uneven surfaces. Should it be taken by surprise or by force and removed

girdle

katy chiton

from its rock, the valves even allow the chiton to curl itself up to protect its soft foot. This curling action of the animal earned it the nickname "sea cradle" (a term preferred by John Steinbeck in *Cannery Row*, his classic account of life along the California coast).

No one would accuse a chiton of being rambunctious or even mildly entertaining. You could watch one all day and never see it move an inch, and if you came back the next day you'd be likely to find it in exactly the same place. There are two reasons for this: Most chitons are nocturnal, and most have a "home" spot they return to before the day breaks. Although they lack eyes, many chitons have light-sensitive spots in their shells, and they often spend the daylight hours under stones or in crevices, hiding from the sun.

One of the most common Northwest chitons breaks that rule, however. The Katy or leather chiton, eschewing the customs of chiton society, cruises the rocks any time of the day or night in a shiny, black, leatherlike girdle. One of the most conspicuous chitons on the rocky coast, the Katy is usually one and a half to three inches long but occasionally reaches five inches. Its Latin name, *Katharina tunicata*, honors Lady Katherine Douglas, the naturalist who sent the first specimen of this species to England for study in 1815.

The world's largest chiton is also found in the Pacific Northwest. *Cryptochiton stelleri*—the gumboot, moccasin, or giant Pacific chiton— grows to fourteen inches and has been described as looking like a wandering meatloaf. The Latin *Crypto* refers to its hidden valves, which are completely covered

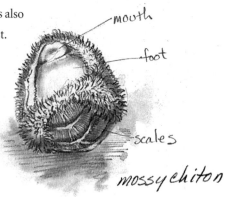

mouth

foot

scales

mossy chiton

by a tough, grainy girdle. The species name *stelleri* honors another early naturalist, Georg Steller (also the eponym of the Steller's jay and Steller's sea lion). The gumboot chiton is brown or reddish brown and is usually found below the low-tide mark.

The mossy chiton (*Mopalia muscosa*) is another relatively common chiton, found under rocks or in crevices. It can grow to nearly four inches, although it's often smaller. Short, stiff hairs on the girdle give this chiton a mossy appearance. The animal is brown, dark olive, or greenish gray, and the eight valves sometimes have a whitish stripe down their centers—as well as small barnacles, algae, or other hitchhikers. Mossy chitons are said to have "teeth of iron," because their radulas, or rasping, file-like tongues, contain magnetite, an oxide of iron. Not only is the radula especially hard, it can be picked up with a magnet.

All chitons use their radulas to scrape food off the rocks. Leaving its home spot, usually under cover of night and/or tide, the animal creeps about, clearing a path as it eats its way through a film of algae. Many chitons are vegetarians, but some also consume minute animals. The rising sun will find most chitons back home, hunkering down for the day. The only time in its life this creature shows a little wanderlust is when it is very young.

Male chitons release sperm, which in most species is then drawn inside the female's mantle cavity (the space between the shell and the soft body) along with the water she draws in for respiration. The fertilized eggs then flow out of the mantle cavity, and the developing young are free-swimming for a brief period before they find a home and begin their sedentary lives.

It's apparently a life that suits them: fossil records show that chitons have remained essentially unchanged for five hundred million to six hundred million years. And, as the variety and abundance of chitons found in the Northwest proves, that life is especially good on the West Coast.

Acorn Barnacles

Latin names: *Balanus glandula; Chthamalus dalli*

Description: Hard, sometimes sharp shell-like plates form a little hummock that houses the animal; large settlements often cover rocks in the tidal zone.
Balanus glandula: usually grayish, grows to about ½ inch in diameter;
Chthamalus dalli: usually brownish, grows to about ¼ inch.

Habitat: Beach rocks, floats, driftwood, pilings, etc., according to species.

My college marine biology classmates and I were unimpressed with barnacles. Sure, we noted their regular occurrence at the various beaches we visited, identified them by species, and dutifully described them in our notebooks. But compared to the snapping crabs, harpoon-flinging anemones, and neon-tipped nudibranchs we were finding, the barnacles were too dull and stodgy to hold our interest.

Nevertheless, our professor, Pete Taylor, decided that we would observe them during one of our lab sessions. He collected

rocks covered with the two species we'd seen most often, the little brown *Chthamalus dalli* and the bigger, grayish *Balanus glandula*. We trained the eyes of our dissecting microscopes on the barnacles, and noted how their shell-like plates overlapped and the characteristic way the four inner plates closed tightly together—those of *C. dalli* in the form of a cross and those of *B. glandula* forming a particular wavy line. It may have been science, but it was not exactly riveting.

Then Pete supplied beakers of fresh seawater and told us to simulate an incoming tide. As we poured the water over the barnacles, they came to life. The inner plates of the submerged fortresses opened, and feathery plumes called cirri extended from each and waved about. Then the cirri abruptly withdrew and the plates once more snapped shut. A moment later, the barnacles opened and again extended the graceful plumes.

We noticed differences between the two species, and scribbled them in our notebooks. The plumes of *B. glandula* curled downward like thin fingers grabbing fistfuls of water; *C. dalli*'s delicate digits spread out and pivoted right and left before dipping back into their shell. Across the broad expanse of the magnified rocks, barnacles repeatedly popped open and shut like tiny jack-in-the-boxes, just as they did with every tide, twice a day. The unexpected animation of the barnacles animated us students too— even thrilled us, giving us a glimpse of how much happens in the natural world to which we are oblivious. And that was before the first wandering barnacle penis poked out of its shell— a sight that further impressed my college class.

Soon more of the surprisingly long, slender probes were reaching into their neighbors' shells in an attempt to release sperm before those plates snapped shut again. Because barnacles are hermaphroditic (having both female and male sex organs), an animal in the process of being impregnated might have its own penis out snaking around the neighborhood. We took copious notes during that lab class.

But you don't need a laboratory or a dissecting microscope to watch the feeding and sexual antics of barnacles. You need only a little patience and a good location where you can observe these little crustaceans underwater—while staying safely away from the waves yourself. The cirri you'll see unfurling act like a net to catch drifting plankton. When they disappear back into the shell, the minuscule food bits are scraped off into the mouthparts, and the cirri roll out again to grab another bite.

Most barnacles hold their fertilized eggs within their shells until the larvae hatch and are released. The larvae swim away and eventually seek a place to settle. Each little creature has a sophisticated ability to sense and test the substrate in an attempt to find just the right spot. Once it attaches, it cannot relocate, so this decision is crucial to its chance of survival. Having made its choice, the larva secretes a cement from glands at the base of its first antennae and glues its head to the substrate. It then begins building the shell-like walls that will encase and protect it and from which the cirri will extend at feeding time. The nineteenth-century scientist Louis Agassiz compared those cirri with the legs of other crustaceans. He wrote that the barnacle is a shrimplike animal that stands on its head and uses its legs to kick food into its mouth. And there's nothing staid or boring about that.

Shrimp

Latin names: *Archaeomysis* spp.; *Heptacarpus* spp.; *Pandalus danae*; *Callianassa* spp.

Description: From less than ¹/₂ inch to 5 inches in length, depending on species; slender bodies; long antennae; jointed legs; may have pincers.

Habitat: Various species can be found in wave wash, sandy mud, estuaries, or tide pools.

Many species of shrimp inhabit Pacific Northwest waters, and some of the most common sport lively, descriptive names such as ghost, opossum, broken-back and coonstriped shrimp. The opossums (*Archaeomysis* spp.) are not true shrimp, but they are closely related and are shrimplike. They can be found jetting about the wash zone of the waves, although you might be most apt to spot them, as my family did, after you wade into the cold waves to collect water for sandcastle making. We found many dozen of these tiny, nearly transparent creatures zipping around in my daughter's big blue bucket. They are called "opossum" shrimp because, like those mammals, the females carry their eggs in special pouches on their abdomens.

It's also sometimes possible to find opossums in a rocky tide pool, but the most common shrimp there is the broken-back (*Heptacarpus* spp.). These half-inch to inch-long shrimp can be recognized by the sharp bend in their abdomens for which they're named—if you can manage to spot one at all. Broken-backs tend to hide among strips of seaweed, blending in amazingly well with in their background. They are covered with tiny dots of many colors, and by controlling the size of these dots they can appear tinged green, white, or brown, or covered with speckles and patches of various colors.

The larger coon-stripe shrimp (*Pandalus danae*) don't change color but can also be hard to pick out from their seabed or eelgrass background. They can grow to five inches long and are brightly colored, with brown, red, and white stripes. The stripes earned them comparison with raccoons and led to their common name. Like other shrimp, they are fastidious little crustaceans and use specialized brushes called *setae* on their legs to groom themselves. Also like some other shrimp, coon-stripes start life as males but become females as they mature, passing through an intersexual stage at two to three years old. Because they are females for the last one to two years of their lives, all of the large specimens of this commercially important species are female.

One of the Pacific Northwest's subterranean shrimp is the ghost shrimp (*Callianassa* spp.), which grows to about three inches. It's so ghostly that its organs can be seen inside its transparent pinkish orange or pinkish gray body. This shrimp burrows industriously for two good reasons: shelter and food. It digs with its mouthparts and hauls the loose particles up to the surface in a sort of basket formed by its legs. Both sexes sport one large claw (the male's can be nearly as long as his body), which they use to push the muddy sand out of the way. Their homes can be recognized on mud flats by the small piles outside each hole. Each burrow has at least two openings and a number of side branches, with wider areas that enable the shrimp to turn around.

The ghost digs down two feet or deeper, collecting food bits to eat as it goes. In the course of its excavations, it mixes the organic debris collected on the top level down into the substrate, creating a never-ending food supply. (This dynamic mining can wreak havoc in an oyster farmer's deliberately placed cultures, however, quickly covering and destroying them.)

At the beach, you can find shrimp with big claws, minuscule ones, or none. You can find shrimp that are far-ranging and ones that are homebodies. You can find shrimp with differing habits and habitats, ones with colorful bodies and ones with colorful names. The Pacific Northwest does not scrimp on shrimp.

Brittle Stars

Latin names: *Ophiopholis aculeata* (daisy brittle star); *Amphipholis occidentalis* (burrowing brittle star); *A. squamata* (small or dwarf brittle star)

Description: Central disk ½ to 3 inches in diameter, distinct from arms; five arms relatively long and thin.

Habitat: Crevices and under rocks in rocky tide pools; offshore, on sea bottom and on seaweed holdfasts.

Unlike the big, bold sea stars, brittle stars are small and delicate, and more likely to be found hiding under a rock than conspicuously clinging to one. Brittle stars are not considered sea stars, and there are important differences between the closely related groups. Brittle stars lack pedicellariae, the tiny jawed stalks that keep sea stars clean of detritus. And although, like sea stars, they have small tube feet studding their undersides, the dainty brittle stars do not use them for locomotion. Instead, they move about by writhing their sinuous arms, two pulling and three pushing in the direction they want to go. The tube feet are used for respiration, as tactile organs, and in feeding.

Brittle stars are also commonly differentiated from another group, the very similar serpent stars, by their mode of defense. At the slightest provocation they will drop arm segments or entire arms—hence the name "brittle." A curious beachcomber who picks up a brittle star can end up holding just the central disk as the startled animal drops arms one after another. (This defense mechanism works better when a hungry fish grabs a single arm and the mostly intact brittle star is able to escape.) The star's arms are later regenerated.

The Pacific Northwest's most common animal of this type is the daisy brittle star, *Ophiopholis aculeata*, which can be found tucked under rocks or crammed into crevices in tide pools. The central disk, less than an inch in diameter, is shaped like a stubby star. It is intricately, often beautifully, mottled with tan and dark or bright red, although markings of grays, white, yellows, oranges, and browns have also been seen. The arms, up to two inches long and covered with stout spines, extend from between the blunt points of the disk and are banded with the two alternating colors.

A star with a more circular disk and much longer arms is the burrowing brittle star, *Amphipholis occidentalis*. These can occasionally be found under rocks in tide pools with sandy bottoms. (Daisy brittle stars prefer tide pools without sand or gravel.) Scuba divers who know to examine muddy sand seafloors and check kelp holdfasts may find them—and may find them in abundance, since they tend to cluster together. Burrowing stars are a mottled gray, and their long arms are strikingly out of proportion with the small disk. The entire animal can measure over a foot across, while its disk is only a half-inch in diameter.

Brittle stars typically burrow down into the sand and then lift their long arms above the sand to capture food. They eat detritus and tiny single-celled plants called diatoms, snagging them with mucus secreted by their arms. A brittle star's digestive organs, unlike those of sea stars, do not extend into the arms, nor can it extrude its stomach. Instead, fine hairs convey the diatoms down the arms and into the creature's mouth. A brittle star's small disk contains both its digestive and its reproductive organs.

Individuals of most species release either sperm or eggs, which meet and mingle in the water, producing swimming young that can settle far from their parents. The small or dwarf brittle star (*A. squamata*) is an interesting exception; our smallest common brittle star broods its young. The female's eggs are held in openings near the base of her arms. The male's sperm enters these slits, and the resulting embryos develop inside the pockets. The mother may brood as many as twenty-five young, which eventually crawl out and disperse. This species is bioluminescent—able to emit a glowing light. The small brittle star is mostly gray, measures up to three inches across, including a disk diameter of a quarter of an inch, and can be found in shallow, muddy water.

Unlike the brazen sea stars, brittle stars make a tide pool visitor hunt to find them. If you have the good luck to uncover one, remember that it's best admired where it lies. It doesn't take much handling before a brittle star decides it is under attack and starts shedding arms left and right . . . and left . . . and . . . .

Hermit Crabs

Latin name: *Pagurus* spp.

Description: Body to about 1½ inches, depending on species; much of body hidden inside an appropriated snail shell; front legs visible; two claws, the right larger than the left; stalked eyes.

Habitat: Rocky shore tide pools, gravel beaches; also offshore to more than 50 feet deep.

If any crab could be called endearing, the hermit crab would be. They just don't seem as irritable or menacing as other crabs—at least toward people. We can pick them up by their shell-houses with impunity.

But if hermits don't seem crabby, it may be because they are not true crabs. Hermits' antennae are positioned differently from those of true crabs, and their abdominal legs are reduced in number and size. For that matter, they're hardly "hermits" either; these little crustaceans are actually rather gregarious.

One of the delightful things about hermit crabs is the surprise of an unexpected resident tucked inside a snail's shell. It was once thought that hermits evicted their shell's original occupant by devouring it, gaining meal and house at once, but studies have shown that they do not eat such large prey. They are, however, particularly sensitive to the scent of dead gastropods, so once someone else has done the evicting, they can track their way to a potential new home.

Finding suitable lodging is a lifelong occupation for hermits, and housing shortages can limit populations. Their soft, coiled abdomens require protection but, as they molt and grow, they must abandon their old, tight-fitting shells. A hermit appraises a new place with the scrutiny of a housing inspector. It grabs the shell with its claws, hefts it and repeatedly turns it around, feels deep inside the cavity with antennae, and cleans out any debris found therein. After much ado, if the place is acceptable, the hermit abruptly pulls its vulnerable abdomen out of the old home and slides quickly into the new. Through evolution, hermits have lost some legs, and the final two pairs are modified to hook onto the shell—helping, along with the abdomen's coil, to secure the animal in place.

Safely ensconced in its hand-me-down home, a hermit crab spends its time scavenging plant and animal debris, tussling with other hermit crabs, or looking for a mate. A male hermit crab has only a brief opportunity to mate with a female: he must time it to coincide with her molt. Therefore, when he finds a female during breeding season, the male grasps the opening of her shell with his small left claw and may lug her around for days. If, as he's biding his time and dragging her about, another male dares to approach, the enraged suitor will ward him off with his large claw. (Hermit crabs are often described as pugnacious, and they do seem happy to drop everything to fight over females, food, or furnishings—but most of their brouhaha is carefully choreographed. Signals are given and respected, and for all the uproar no one ever seems to get hurt.)

When the female finally molts, their

mating is a hasty affair. Both animals pull nearly out of their shells, and the male quickly deposits sperm on the female's abdomen. She later uses this to fertilize her eggs as they are laid. The female retains two degenerated appendages on the left side of her abdomen, and these "swimmerets" are used to carry the eggs. She waves the swimmerets about from time to time, drawing fresh seawater with its oxygen into her shell. Eventually the hatched young leave the protection of their mother's shell and begin their own adventures.

Different species of hermit crabs prefer specific habitats and even particular types of shells. But all spend their days trundling about in their appropriated mobile homes. And all, despite their puckish inclination to fight one another, strike most beachcombers as amusing—even charming—little crabs.

Rockweed

Latin name: *Fucus gardneri*

Description: To 12 inches long; yellowish green to olive-green when wet; can appear almost black when dry; plant branches at regular intervals of 1 to 2 inches; prominent midrib runs down center of flattened, lobed branches; branch tips may be swollen and warty.

Habitat: Upper areas of tide pools.

We think of most seaweed as living, appropriately, in the sea, but this alga's common name of rockweed says it all. Rather than stretching up from ocean depths, it hangs from tide pool rocks in thick moist curtains. Rockweed is found along the coast and within Puget Sound; it is one of the Northwest's most common and most often seen seaweeds.

Each plant is secured to its rock by a disk-shaped holdfast. Unlike most land plants, which can photosynthesize only through their leaves, rockweed can take in the sun's energy throughout its entire body. It is a hardy seaweed, able to withstand extreme changes in temperature and salinity levels and loss of moisture each day. In fact, it holds in moisture so well that it creates a microhabitat used by small creatures who escape the heat of a sunny day beneath the plant's fronds.

There is evidence, however, that rockweed may wage a quiet sort of war against the creatures that would grow up to graze on it. The seaweed releases tannins that can kill planktonic crustaceans that land in its tide pool. As rockweed ages, its ability to create the tannins used in the chemical warfare diminishes. This may allow grazers such as sea urchins to clear away the older plants, making way for a new generation of pioneer seaweed.

Rockweed doesn't share the complicated reproduction scheme of bull kelp and most other seaweeds. Its simplified version bypasses the asexual generation with its intermediate microscopic stage, and its fertilized eggs develop directly into young plants. When rockweed is mature and ready to reproduce, the tips of its fronds inflate into bulbs. These give the plant its other two common names, bladder wrack and popping wrack (when squeezed, the bulbs make a popping sound, squirting water through tiny pores). The bulbs develop small bumps, where the gametes (sex cells) are stored. Female organs each hold eight eggs, while male organs produce sperm packets, each of which contains sixty-four sperms.

As the appropriate time nears for their release, the bulbs dry and begin to shrink. The plant doesn't simply jettison the gametes into any old wave-bashing tide, however. Incredibly, it waits for the daytime low tide, when the water is relatively calm. Rockweed might "recognize" daylight via its photosynthetic cells, but how it determines low tide is not yet understood. At any rate, the plant shoots its gametes into the water through tiny holes. After the gametes are released, the floating eggs secrete a pheromone that attracts the swimming sperm. These gather around the much larger egg, attach themselves, and begin to spin their way in. When one sperm manages to fertilize the egg, the rest take off in hot pursuit of another available egg. As it is carried off by the waves, the fertilized egg begins developing immediately. If it is to survive, the resulting tiny young plant must eventually be thrust up onto an appropriate spot by the waves. There it develops a holdfast and, if it escapes grazing by snails, sea urchins, chitons, and limpets, can grow to be a foot or more long.

The abundance of this alga on the Northwest Coast proves the success both of its reproductive strategy and of its coastline lifestyle. Like all seaweeds, rockweed lives its life associated with salt water—but demands it on the rocks.

Tube Worms

Latin names: *Serpula vermicularis* (fan worm); *Eudistylia vancouveri* and *Schizobranchia insignis* (feather-duster or plume worms); *Spirorbis* spp.

Description: To 20 inches long, depending on species; visible parts of worm feathery, colorful tentacles extending from head; hard white tube or leathery tube encloses rest of body.

Habitat: Coastal shorelines; depending on species, on floats, pilings, floating docks, on shells and seaweed, on sides and undersides of rocks; in tide pools, estuaries, and offshore.

We don't usually think of worms as pretty creatures, but fan worms and feather-duster worms certainly are. Or at least the delicate, feathery portions of them that we can see are lovely.

The worm sometimes called the calcareous tube worm or fan worm (*Serpula vermicularis*) builds its home from lime that it somehow extracts from seawater, creating a hard white tube that protects its soft body. The tube grows longer as the worm ages (fine rings on the shell show the gradual additions). The homes may be nearly straight or may curl or meander over rock (or whatever the animal has attached itself to). Although the tube may be as long as four inches, the worm inside maxes out at two and one-half inches long.

Like its relative the common earthworm, the fan worm is pinkish or reddish-orange and segmented. Unlike the earthworm, it unfurls two gorgeous feathery tentacles, or cirri, in order to eat and breathe. The spiraling cirri, which can be brilliant red or orange and often have white bands, wave about, taking in food and oxygen. Tiny hairlike cilia on the cirri set up a rhythmic pulse that helps to pull in minute particles of food. Once the particles have contacted the cirri, they are conveyed via mucus and cilia to the creature's mouth.

Another cirrus plume has been modified to a funnel shape that is often compared to a golf tee. If the tube worm senses danger, it snaps back into its shell and this golf tee is the last cirrus to retract. The tee is an operculum, or lid, that seals the worm inside. The operculum is as red as the rest of the cirri, so each closed tube-worm home seems to be sealed off with a little bright-red door.

Relatives called feather-duster or plume worms (*Eudistylia vancouveri* and *Schizobranchia insignis*) live in leathery or parchmentlike tubes. These live in much the same way as do fan worms, but they can grow much larger. The tube of *E. vancouveri* can be twenty inches long, sprouting flowerlike cirri that measure two inches across. Their cirri can be white to green to deep maroon or purple.

Another worm, known as *Spirorbis*, is less impressive, but only because of its small size. These worms are more easily overlooked, although they are quite common. They build their homes in tiny, tight spirals about a tenth of an inch or less in diameter, and they favor out-of-the-way places like the undersides of rocks or seaweed. Like the other tube worms, *Spirorbis* has brightly colored red cirri. One of the ways in which it differs from other tube worms is in its sex life. Most tube worms are either male or female and, in season, send out sperm or eggs to mingle and fertilize in the water (although some species brood the young in the female's tube). But *Spirorbis* is both male and female simultaneously. Curiously, the front part of its abdomen is female, while its posterior end is male. In some species, the operculum has a special cavity that serves as a brood pouch for larvae.

The beaches and waters of the Pacific Northwest are squirming with all kinds of worms. The Northwest hosts so many species that guidebooks dedicated to worms alone could be written. But of all the worms you're likely to run into, surely some of the loveliest and most graceful are the tube worms who daily perform their food-gathering fan dances.

Black Oystercatcher

Latin name: *Haematopus bachmani*

Description: To 18 inches; long orange-red beak; yellow eye surrounded by red ring; dark plumage; pinkish legs.

Habitat: On rocky shores and islands; rarely on sandy and cobble beaches.

Birds that dine on shellfish have developed a variety of ways to get to the encased meaty bits. Scoters simply swallow a mussel whole and let their muscular gizzards do the work; gulls take a clam up into the air and drop it on a rock to crack it open. Black oystercatchers rely on sneak attacks.

The long-beaked shorebird strolls along the rocky coast, or sometimes wades in water up to its belly, looking for any mussel that has opened its shell slightly to breathe and feed. Finding a mussel in this vulnerable position, the oystercatcher abruptly thrusts its bright, chisel-like beak between the mollusk's shells. It was long thought that the bird severed the strong muscles that clamp the mollusk's two shells shut, but apparently the swift stroke of the oystercatcher's bill paralyzes the mussel's nervous system instead.

A similar fate awaits unlucky crabs. Finding one of these, the oystercatcher flips it onto its back and kills it with a blow to the center of the nervous system. Despite its name, the oystercatcher of the Pacific Coast doesn't catch many oysters. (The region's small native oyster, *Ostrea lurida*, is not usually found in large numbers.) The Northwest bird gained its name through the activities of the American oystercatcher, found in other regions. The black oystercatcher is more apt to eat limpets, chitons, and barnacles, in addition to mussels and crabs. On its rare forays to sandy beaches, it also probes about for worms.

In spring the oystercatcher's attention turns to courtship. An enamored couple can put on quite a display: the two bow to one another and take off in noisy flying chases, their loud calls ringing out over the sound of the surf. Pair bonds are long-term, and the couple often uses the same nest site year after year. The female lays two eggs in late May or June, usually in a shallow depression or on beach gravel above the high-tide line.

Because they are ground nesters, oystercatchers are especially vulnerable to beachcombers and their dogs, and to boaters who visit outcroppings and small islands. The birds are sensitive to disturbance and may abandon their nest, although they would probably attempt another clutch.

The parents take turns incubating the eggs. The returning adult, as if being thoughtful, relieves its hungry mate during low tide, when meals are easiest to find. The eggs hatch after twenty-four to twenty-nine days, and the young are able to run at three days old. Only two days later they begin feeding themselves, catching insects in their bills. Although they get off to a fast start, it will take many months before the young are truly able to take care of themselves. The oystercatcher's sneak-attack method of drilling into an animal's nervous system takes some time to properly learn. The young sometimes stay with their parents for nearly a year, ensuring that they get enough food while they're studying the proper technique.

Eventually the young oystercatchers are able to fend for themselves and leave the sheltering care of their parents. Having survived the ravens, crows, and gulls that like to snatch eggs, bumbling beachcombers, and an extended adolescence, the newly emancipated oystercatchers may live for more than thirty years. They never stray far from their birthing areas, however. Instead of migrating, oystercatchers form small flocks in winter and usually stay within thirty miles of their breeding grounds. Their red-rimmed eyes may give them the look of wild party-goers, but black oyster-catchers are really monogamous homebodies.

Tidepool Sculpin

Latin name: *Oligocottus maculosus*

Description: To about 3½ inches long; large head and front fins, body tapers to tail; not scaly; usually a mottled gray, but variable.

Habitat: Rocky tide pools, exposed or protected.

Amongst all the curious creatures found in a typical tide pool, there is liable to be only one that has a backbone: the tidepool sculpin, or tidepool johnny. This little fish is easy to overlook, however. At a maximum length of three and a half inches and cleverly camouflaged, it blends in splendidly with its background.

There are other sculpins and other small fish that inhabit the rocky pools, but one of the most commonly found is the tidepool sculpin. It is generally described as "ugly" because of its large head and mouth and disproportionately tapering body. Its pectoral fins (the two front ones) are relatively large and shaped like fans. The fish not only uses these to scuttle around on the bottom of the pool but can also stretch them up and sideways to make itself look more imposing or threatening. In about twenty minutes, this sculpin can change its color to blend in with a new background, becoming various shades of red, brown, green, or gray. The only constant in its coloration seems to be a small spot of white near the base of the tail, although there are also often dark or whitish saddles on its back.

Like all tide pool creatures, the sculpin is extremely tolerant of changes in the temperature, salinity, and oxygen content of its pool. The sun not only heats up a small pool, it also evaporates some water, making the remaining water saltier. Rain, on the other hand, dilutes the seawater. Despite a tide pool's apparent peaceful stability, the conditions within it can change dramatically between tidal visits.

When the tide is up, the sculpin usually leaves its home pool on feeding excursions, especially in summer. It tours around the vicinity, seeking shrimp, smaller fish, and crabs, which it captures with a short burst of speed and a quick gulp of its large mouth. By low tide, the wayfaring sculpin has returned to its home pool or a nearby one. Scientists curious about this homing behavior have determined that the fish finds its way back by smell. Sculpins high in the upper intertidal zone can be homebodies, however, rarely venturing out but simply waiting for edible goodies to be washed into their pools.

One good reason to leave home is for reproduction, which occurs from November through May. Some kind of copulation may be involved in their spawning, and a male of this type of sculpin is amply endowed with a papilla or "fish penis." The females deposit small clusters of adhesive eggs. These are green or maroon and are sometimes scattered in beds of mussels or barnacles.

In addition to sculpins, you may find two other types of fish in a tide pool. One type is blenny eels—a term that refers collectively to the prickle-backs and gunnels. These fish look like little eels and are from three to five inches long. They can sometimes be found by lifting tide pool rocks. (Whenever you move a seashore rock, whether in a pool or on the beach, it is important to the creatures surrounding it that you replace it in exactly the same position you found it.) When flushed from its hiding place, a blenny eel slithers about like a snake.

The aptly named clingfish, like the blenny eels, can be found underneath rocks, especially ones with smooth undersides. The clingfish grows to about six inches and is tadpole-shaped, with a wide body and tapering tail. It attaches itself to rocks (or even your hand) with a surprisingly strong suction created by its pelvic and pectoral fins.

Looking into a tide pool, a little fish will be the sole fellow vertebrate that you're liable to find. When it comes to seashore life, invertebrates rule the pool.

Mink

Latin name: *Mustela vison*

Description: To 28 inches long, with half of the length being tail; cylindrical, brown fur-covered body, usually with white patch under chin and perhaps on chest; short legs; somewhat bushy tail.

Habitat: Near rivers, marshes, lakes, estuaries, and along rocky beaches.

You might expect to see mink worn at a swanky big city party rather than on the beach—unless you've encountered it on the living animal. Mink are a kind of weasel that prefer watery habitats. They are carnivores and will take just about any animal they can subdue, often with a bite to the neck. Inland, their diet includes muskrat, fish, crayfish, and frogs. When mink are beach dwellers, the specialty on the menu is fresh seafood: they forage in tide pools, dining on sea urchins and crustaceans, especially crabs. In season, they claim the eggs of Northwest-breeding shorebirds such as oystercatchers.

Though it's not unusual to see mink in the daytime, they are primarily active during the night. They spend much of their time patrolling their territory in search of food. The territories, generally linear because they follow the water's edge, vary in size depending on the season and availability of food; males claim a larger area than females. Each animal has a number of dens to choose from and may spend a few nights or many in one before moving on to another. The dens are frequently in a hollow tree or in the earth beneath the roots of a tree. Mink are quite neat in their toilet habits, defecating and urinating only outside their dens.

Like other weasels, mink tend to be loners. Though they are not quite as antisocial as some of their kin, mink who encounter one another can end up in a nasty fight. In addition to fighting tooth and nail, these animals, like their relations the skunks, are equipped with another potent weapon: anal glands under their tails release an ugly, fetid odor that usually lingers far longer than the disturbance that caused its release.

But as springtime approaches, even loners become interested in company. Beginning in late February, a male roams farther than usual in pursuit of a female. Once found, she is unwilling to submit meekly to his advances, which include grabbing her by the neck with his teeth. Copulation between minks looks more like a hurly-burly brawl. But if the female is receptive, she will eventually move her tail to the side and allow him to mate with her. They may copulate more than once, but during the rest periods in between, he never lets go of her neck. When he finally does, perhaps as much as three hours later, it is the signal that copulation is finished. Either may mate once or twice more with different

partners. This, combined with delayed implantation of the eggs, means that female mink may carry young who have different fathers.

The expectant mother enlarges a section of a den and lines it with feathers, fur, and grasses. She generally births four young, though the number may vary from two to eight. Her tiny babies are just one or two inches long, but they grow quickly. By five weeks they are weaned, and in eight weeks they are capturing their own prey. The family stays together until the end of summer, when the young disperse in search of their own water-bordered territories. They may wander farther inland to a lake or river, or choose an area along the coast. Mink fur certainly looks chic at the beach—when it's still on its original owner.

Madrone

Latin name: *Arbutus menziesii*

Description: To 80 feet high; thick, leathery oblong leaves to about 5 inches, usually with smooth margins, but sometimes serrated on quickly growing young trees; peeling reddish brown bark reveals smooth green underbark; reddish orange berrylike fruits in fall.

Habitat: Often found on sunny, rocky slopes and cliffs; requires well-drained soil.

Madrone, or madrona, has been called the tree that sheds its bark instead of its leaves. It's one of those trees that proves the term "evergreen" does not always mean "conifer." Madrone is a broadleaf tree that fits the definition of evergreen: it holds onto its leaves for more than one season. (Larch trees do the opposite: they drop all their needles every year and are deciduous conifers.)

Madrones hang onto those leaves until about midsummer, when the new leaves are ready to replace them. The thick leaves, which show a family resemblance to those of rhododendron, turn deep red before they finally give up and fall heavily to the ground. The new leaves are glossy dark green and whitish underneath.

The tree's flowers appear in spring, before the leaves drop. The individual bell-shaped blossoms, which have been compared to lilies-of-the-valley, grow in large clusters at the ends of the branches. The numerous little creamy-white flowers give off a sweet fragrance that calls in honeybees, and sometimes hummingbirds, to mine their nectar. Once the birds and bees have inadvertently pollinated the flowers, each blossom develops into a pea-sized green fruit. In autumn the little fruits turn reddish orange, resembling miniature oranges, and unless gobbled up by birds they will remain on the tree into December. The birds who eat the fruits, carrying the seeds off in their bellies to be disseminated later, include quail, pileated woodpeckers, and especially band-tailed pigeons.

As if its leaves, flowers, and fruits were not colorful enough, the madrone's bark puts on a show of its own. The most intriguing thing about madrone is its appealing, peeling bark. The reddish brown outer bark cracks and curls into strips, revealing a lovely, smooth, chartreuse under-bark. Its strip-tease performance makes madrone the Gypsy Rose Lee of trees—and tempts voyeuristic humans to peel off yet more of those inviting chips and flakes. The green underbark will gradually take on a ruddy reddish brown hue before it, too, is ready to peel off. Older trees grow a crinkly gray bark at their bases, but the young bark on their branches still shows the wonderfully contrasting madrone colors.

Although they are largely associated with rocky places, madrones show their best growth in well-drained areas where they are not crowded out by conifers. There they can grow to eighty feet tall and live for two centuries. One venerable individual in California, called the Council Madrona by settlers, once served as an important meeting place for Indian tribes who forged agreements under its spreading branches.

The name *madroño* was given to the tree by early Spanish explorers who noted its resemblance to a related Mediterranean species, the "madro." Over time, the name has changed to "madrona" or "madrone" in the United States, while British Columbians generally prefer "arbutus."

John Muir, that consummate naturalist and near-druid, came across the tree in his travels and wrote: "The madrona, clad in thin, smooth, red and yellow bark, with big, glossy leaves, seems in the dark coniferous forests of Washington and Vancouver Island like some lost wanderer from the magnolia groves of the South." Most broadleaf evergreens do prefer a warmer year-round climate; how fortunate for us that the colorful madrone makes its home in the Pacific Northwest.

Northern Harrier

Latin name: *Circus cyaneus*

Description: Female: larger than male (to about 21 inches); brown above, light buff below with brown streaks. Male: gray above with black wing tips, mostly white below. Both sexes have conspicuous white rump patch.

Habitat: Open country including wet meadows, dry grasslands, coastal headlands.

The northern harrier is one of those birds that can be recognized almost more by what it's doing than by how it looks. Any large bird cruising extremely low over a meadow or an open grassy area during daylight hours is likely to be a harrier. A telltale patch of white near the tail can quickly confirm the identification.

Of course, other hawks and other large birds hunt in the same type of habitat, but they are more likely to swoop or stoop (dive) to the kill. Hunting harriers patrol the area with purpose, crisscrossing the field, wings usually held in a slight V, head down, sometimes rocking slightly from side to side. They rarely fly higher than seven feet and often seem to be skimming the tops of vegetation.

There's a good reason for the difference in their hunting technique: as they glide over the grass-tops, harriers are listening for squeaks and rustles. Unlike others in their sharp-eyed hawk family, harriers rely more on their hearing than on their vision to locate prey. A "facial disk" (like that of owls) helps: the feathers around the harrier's eyes and beak create a concave surface, something like that of a satellite dish, which directs sound into the harrier's ears.

Once the bird has pinpointed the source of the sound, it sometimes hovers before dropping onto the vole or mouse. Should the varmint escape, or realize prematurely that it is about to become someone's dinner, the hawk will chase it, using its tail as rudder to make sharp twists and turns, paralleling in the air the rodent's winding path below.

Voles and mice are the harrier's main prey, especially in winter. But the birds are also known to take ducklings, frogs, crawdads, snakes, and large insects such as grasshoppers. The state of the local vole population seems to determine whether a breeding male harrier will be monogamous or polygynous. If the voles are having a good year and are numerous, the harrier is apt to have more than one mate; when the hunting is easy, he can feed two or sometimes even three families instead of just one.

The male charms a female with his aerial displays, so different from his usual careful quartering of a field. He rockets skyward, seems almost to stall, and plummets toward the ground, looping suddenly upward once more. The coloration differences between the male and female are so pronounced that he would almost seem to be performing for a bird of another species. Female harriers are mostly brown, while males are mostly gray, although both sport the white rump patch.

The prospective parents build a rather flimsy nest out of sticks and grass, usually on the ground. The female lays an average of five eggs, and as she incubates them over the next month or so, the male brings her food. He usually drops these tidbits near her and the female catches them on the wing, but sometimes there is an aerial claw-to-claw exchange. Once the chicks are hatched, he hunts for the entire family. When the young are fledged, the whole family may hunt together for a time. Outside of the breeding season, twenty to fifty harriers may roost together on the ground.

These birds were once known by the common name "marsh hawk," although they are also found in dry grasslands and any other open country. But the name "harrier" is easy to remember if you think of the way they "harry" voles, chasing down their zigzagging prey.

Sitka Spruce

Latin name: *Picea sitchensis*

Description: To over 300 feet high; scaly bark purplish gray or reddish brown; needles stiff and prickly, arranged singly in spirals around twig; cylindrical cones 2 to 3½ inches long hang down from branches, scales thin and papery.

Habitat: Moist or wet soils of the coast, areas of high rain and fog.

It can be said that the fog of the Pacific Coast makes music. And that the fog helped win World Wars I and II. These things can be claimed because the wood of Sitka spruce has gone into countless musical instruments and many airplanes—and because the tree requires the fog's high humidity to grow.

This also explains why the Northwest's largest Sitka spruces are in the fogbound Hoh, Queets, and Quinault valleys of Olympic National Park, and why the tree is rarely found more than a dozen miles from the coast. Remarkably, the ocean's salt spray also aids this tree. The needles of Sitka spruce, unlike those of any other conifer, can absorb minerals such as calcium and phosphorus directly from the spray.

Sitka spruce was in great demand during the two World Wars. Its wood, lightweight yet strong, was made into airplane frames in the United States, England, and France. During the First World War, the ten thousand U.S. soldiers of the Spruce Division logged the forests of the Pacific Coast. A tremendous number of trees fell in the quest for boards that met the blemish- and knot-free, straight-grained specifications necessary for early aircraft. The search for those boards was called "the jewel trade of the lumber business."

The wood's remarkable strength-to-weight ratio, the highest of any lumber, still makes it the ideal choice for ladders, scaffolding, folding bleachers, racing-boat shells, and experimental aircraft. But Sitka spruce's gift of resonance is the reason musicians prize it. After tapping and listening to the wood, an experienced carver enriches the world by turning Sitka spruce into violin, guitar, and bass tops, harp frames, and sound boards for pianos.

Other uses for Sitka spruce are more ancient. Elk and deer browse the foliage, at least until the tender new needles turn prickly. Chickadees and other songbirds eat the seeds. Native peoples used the thin rootlets when weaving baskets and rain hats, caulked boats with the pitch, or chewed it like an aromatic gum, and steeped the inner bark in hot water for a medicinal tea.

Aside from its many uses, Sitka spruce is simply a gigantic, awe-inspiring tree. It is the world's fourth-tallest tree species and the northern Pacific Coast's equivalent of those more southerly giants, the redwoods. Under the best conditions, this spruce can reach over three hundred feet tall and can live to be seven hundred or eight hundred years old. It grows straight, tapering to a skyward point, and may grow thick buttresses at the base to help stabilize its huge old self. Its shallow root system does not require deep humus but does demand plenty of water. A seedling can take hold in moist soil, even on a floodplain or tidal area, a characteristic that earned the tree the early name of "tideland spruce." But because the big bruisers never send down a deep, anchoring taproot, strong winds wreak havoc with them. Big storms can tip over Sitka spruce, pulling their shallow roots right out of the ground.

Gentler winds serve Sitka spruce by helping to disperse its seeds considerable distances from the parent tree. Still, with its demands for water and high humidity, this spruce rarely wanders too far from the coast and its life-giving fog.

Wetlands

Wetlands were once likened to wastelands, but now they're being compared to supermarkets, sponges, nurseries, safe havens—and even kidneys. As scientific understanding of the value of wetlands has expanded, so have the ways in which biologists, naturalists, educators, and journalists try to explain their importance.

But before the comparisons are made, the term "wetlands" requires explanation. It is the umbrella term used to describe areas where the soil is at least periodically inundated or saturated with water. Although the term generally excludes permanent lakes, ponds, rivers, streams, and the ocean, wetlands are often found associated with these larger, deeper bodies of water. The word is not some newfangled attempt to pretty-up the terms "swamp," "bog," or "marsh"; instead, each of these terms is a specific kind of wetland, differentiated by the kinds of plants it supports.

Some types of wetlands support so many different plant and animal species that they're as productive as a tropical rain forest or a coral reef. Wetlands have been called "biological supermarkets" that feed various birds, amphibians, fish, reptiles, insects, and mammals. Some of these animals spend their entire lives within a wetland; others, such as migratory birds, are stop-and-go shoppers that depend on the food and shelter of strategically placed wetlands along their route.

Wetlands are often described as sponges because of their ability to soak up flood waters and release the excess water slowly over time. A river's floodplain is a broad expanse that, most of the year, is relatively dry as the water flows through it in a channel. Heavy rains, spring thaw, or sudden snowmelt periodically cause the river to overflow its banks, inundating the floodplain. So when floodplains and other wetlands near rivers are filled in and built upon, the result can be flooded houses, damaged property, and sometimes loss of human life.

Soggy areas left in their natural state release water slowly, which helps to maintain a stream's flow during drier months. Additionally, these sponge-like wetlands gradually allow the recharging of groundwater and aquifers, from which many communities draw their tap water.

Wetlands associated with estuaries are nurseries—sheltered environments where saltwater fish and shellfish such as crabs begin their life cycles. Many freshwater fish also get their start in wetlands, as do ducks and other bird species. Wetlands are called safe havens because it's estimated that more than forty percent of all federally listed threatened or endangered species rely on them at some point in their lives.

Their similarity to kidneys may not be immediately obvious unless you know that wetlands also act as filters. Studies show that some wetlands are able to absorb the phosphates and nitrates from agricultural use and to purify sewage and storm runoff. Biochemical processes within these ecosystems break down dangerous chemicals into less dangerous ones, and the dense vegetation traps pollutants, which are eventually buried by sediments.

Additionally, wetlands act as storm buffers, stabilize shorelines, and offer recreational activities ranging from birdwatching and wildlife viewing to fishing and hunting. Unfortunately, the many benefits of wetlands have become obvious to us only after we've already destroyed more than fifty percent of America's original wetlands. Of the two hundred and fifteen million acres that existed when the United States was founded, fewer than ninety-nine million remain. Convinced that these areas were worthless or hazardous, we have drained, filled, and paved over wetlands, or used them as community dump sites.

Our current understanding of wetlands is far from complete. But the more scientists learn, and the more our lawmakers and the general public understand, the safer our crowded, creative, sheltering wet places will be.

Western Painted and Pond Turtles

Latin names: *Chrysemys picta bellii* (western painted turtle);
Clemmys marmorata marmorata (western pond turtle)

Description: Western painted turtle: to 10 inches long; thin yellow and red stripes on neck and legs; shell olive or blackish, red at edges; underside yellow, black, and red. Western pond turtle: to 8 inches long; shell dark brown or olive; underside has variable black and/or yellow markings. In both species, male is smaller than female and has longer, wider tail; male painted turtle also has elongated front claws.

Habitat: Marshes, rivers, slow streams, lakes and ponds with aquatic vegetation.

Turtles are both venerable and vulnerable. Venerable because individual turtles are thought to live long lives and also because these reptiles have been around for two hundred and fifty million years and once shared swamps with the dinosaurs. Despite their demonstrated staying power, native turtles are now vulnerable in Washington and Oregon, due to habitat destruction, collection for pets and as food, and predation by introduced species such as the bullfrog and the largemouth bass. Over much of their traditional range, western pond and painted turtles have also been muscled out by red-eared sliders, the turtles that were once commonly sold in pet stores (and apparently also rather commonly released by their former owners into the wild).

Despite their tenuous situation, Northwestern native turtles appear to spend lives of quiet relaxation. In addition to their basking-in-the-sun itinerary, however, turtles have things to do, such as foraging for food. Their diet features spiders, insect larvae, tadpoles, crayfish, and most aquatic plants, including algae and duckweed.

At night, turtles usually sink or swim to the bottom of their ponds to spend the night burrowed in soft mud. This is also where they spend the winter months (western pond turtles also sometimes overwinter on land). As their metabolism idles down, the submerged turtles receive all the oxygen they require through their skin and via their cloacal vents. (This opening, on the underside of the turtle's tail, discharges the turtle's urinary, intestinal, and reproductive products.) After a long winter's nap, turtles are called back to the surface by warmer weather.

Their hormones also awaken in spring. A male painted turtle courts a female by swimming backward in front of her, facing her. He uses the elongated claws on his front feet to gently fan water against her face, and may also occasionally stroke her face with his claws. She may respond by touching his feet with her own, shorter claws. The pair then sinks to the bottom to mate underwater. The male positions himself behind the female, and his penis extends from his cloacal vent and enters the female's vent. (One way to tell male and female turtles apart is that the male's tail is considerably longer and wider in order to accommodate the inverted penis. His vent is also located farther down on his tail;

the female's vent, also on the tail, is usually positioned at the margin of the shell or somewhat inside it.)

The female is able to retain the sperm for years (yes, *years*). When ready to lay her eggs, she leaves the relative safety of the water for what can be a treacherous trip on land. She may travel more than a half-mile away in pursuit of a nesting location. When she's satisfied, she uses her back feet to dig a hole into the soft dirt or sand. Once she has deposited her clutch of (usually four to eight) eggs, her parental duties are complete.

Studies suggest that the gender of the hatchlings is determined by the temperature of the nest (although this has not yet been conclusively confirmed in the native turtles). Warmer nests tend to produce only females; somewhat cooler nests may result in all male young. A fluctuating temperature may produce both sexes. The hatchlings sometimes overwinter in their nest and emerge the following spring. Both as eggs and as hatchlings, they are especially vulnerable to predation by creatures including raccoons, skunks, and snakes. Even after they have survived the journey to a watery home, the hatchlings are easy prey for herons, large fish, other turtles, and especially the introduced bullfrog. People sometimes catch or kill turtles as well, though it is against the law to disturb them.

These native turtles' basic requirement of a muddy-bottomed pond was once easily found in the Pacific Northwest. But as wetlands have increasingly been filled in and paved over, the relatively slow-moving turtles have moved ever more quickly toward extinction.

Cattails

Latin names: *Typha latifolia* (broad-leaved cattail); *T. augustifolia* (narrow-leaved cattail)

Description: 3 to 10 feet tall; stalk topped with spongy, cylindrical spike that emerges green but turns brown; leaves green, long, and slender, sometimes taller than stalk.

Habitat: Still or slow-moving shallow fresh water, in sloughs, ponds, marshes, ditches, and lakes.

A more accurate common name might have compared the brown flowering heads of these wetland plants to cigars, or to sausages—but for sheer charm, "cattails" can't be beat. A wild-plant forager also finds cattails hard to beat in terms of usefulness.

From the pollen formed at the tip of its stalk to the creeping underground stem buried in the muck, much of a cattail is edible. Noted wild-foods enthusiast Euell Gibbons (who once appeared in a television commercial inquiring "Did you ever eat a pine tree?") called cattails "the supermarket of the swamps." By fall those underground stems, called rhizomes, are full of starch intended to see the plant through the winter. Dug up, the rhizomes can be baked, eaten raw, or dried and pulverized into a flour.

The pollen can also be eaten. It comes from male flowers that grow at the very top of the stalk, above the fat stogie-like cylinder of female flowers. The minute flowers of both sexes are green when they first emerge. The slender spike of the male portion is enclosed by a papery sheath that protects the developing pollen grains. When the pollen is mature, the sheath splits open to shower its bounty down on the waiting female flowers below. Breezes help to pollinate neighboring cattails. A forager harvests the pollen by breaking off the male spikes after they turn golden but before the sheaths open. The spikes, boiled and served with butter and salt, can be eaten like miniature corn on the cob. The dried golden pollen can be added to flour to make pancakes, muffins, and bread, or sprinkled into soups and stews to thicken them.

And the cattail's succulent green sprouts that grow from the rhizomes each spring can be eaten raw like celery or cooked like asparagus. The tender white bottoms of leaves can also be nibbled.

Its culinary uses are just the tip of the cattail, however. The female spike is said to stanch bleeding when cut open and laid against a wound. Northwest tribes once made springy mattresses and comfortable kneeling pads for their canoes from cattail stalks. Woven cattail roofs covered their summer houses. The leaves, dried and then soaked, are also excellent weaving material, and have been used for chair seats and mats. The multitudinous downy seeds that develop from the female spike (each plant is estimated to produce two hundred thousand tiny seeds, each with its own wispy parachute) have been used as everything from cradle-board padding to stuffing for quilts, pillows, and life preservers.

Animals use cattails for the same purposes: food and shelter. Muskrats in particular depend on cattails for food, and will stash a pile of the rhizomes in their homes. Geese also eat the carbohydrate- and nutrient-laden rhizomes. Male red-winged blackbirds yodel their eligibility for mating from cattail perches, and females build their cuplike nests in the plants. Many birds use the down as padding or insulation in their nests. (An American coot couple will construct up to nine bulky floating nests, though the female will lay eggs in only one or two of them.) Other birds, including marsh wrens and ducks, make use of the sheltering cattails, as do the usual assortment of water-loving critters like frogs and dragonflies.

A cattail's reason for being is, of course, to make more cattails, but along the way it benefits any number of creatures. Its many uses may not be as well known to people as they once were, but the cattail's unique look and delightful, descriptive name ensure that everyone can still recognize and name it.

Dragonflies and Damselflies

Latin name: Order Odonata; various genera and species

Description: Long, slender insects with four wings; often brilliantly colored, males sometimes more so than females. Dragonflies: large, bulging eyes cover much of head; wings fixed horizontally at right angles to back. Damselflies: eyes on sides of head; wings usually held over top of back when at rest.

Habitat: Usually near water, ponds, streams, rivers, and lakes, but dragonflies can occasionally be found in woodlands or fields miles from water.

*f*ierce dragons and fair damsels live not only in fairy tales but also beside ponds and streams. Dragonflies and damselflies are closely related insects that can generally be distinguished from one another by size (damsels are daintier) and by wing position (dragons' wings are always positioned straight out from their bodies like the wings of a small plane).

Damselflies are not strong fliers, and they tend to stick to the shoreline with its sheltering reeds and vegetation. Dragonflies patrol wide stretches of open water, although they too can be seen along the shoreline. The males of both groups stake out small territories that they defend from other males. If conditions are crowded and they are forced to share territories with other members of their own species, a hierarchy of dominance is established. The males exchange quick signals to confirm their rank—for instance, a raising of the abdomen for dominance, a lowering for subordination.

The dominant male gets first choice of the females who arrive in the territory, ready to mate. But first each male dragonfly must prepare himself for the upcoming festivities. He is in the peculiar predicament of having two reproductive organs located in different parts of his body. The jointed

mating damselflies

penis is situated in the second abdominal segment, just behind his legs, while the sperm is produced at his rear end. Before courting, he bends the tip of his abdomen way up and transfers sperm into a special pouch near the penis. Damselflies must do the same before mating, but most of them wait until after they've seized a female.

Fully loaded and ready for action, the dragonfly hovers into position above a receptive female. He first grabs her with his legs, then bends his abdomen so that claspers on the last segment can reach matching grooves on her neck. Once the claspers attach, he lets go with his legs, and the pair is said to be in tandem. He now flies slightly above and ahead of her, connected tail to neck.

However, her reproductive organs are located at her tail end, while his penis is rather inconveniently far forward on his abdomen. The tantric contortions that ensue are characterized by Howard Ensign Evans in *Life on a Little-Known Planet* as "one of the most bizarre performances to be seen anywhere. Doubtless if a trip to the Kalahari Desert were required to observe it, more publicity would result."

While the pair are in the air, or when they land somewhere, the female bends her abdomen up to reach the male's organ. His tail remains firmly attached to her neck throughout, and the pair's two looping bodies describe a sort of lopsided heart shape. It can be difficult for an observer who doesn't already understand the acrobatics involved to recognize just which abdomen belongs to which insect.

Some species end their attachment with the exchange of sperm, though the male usually hovers nearby as the female lays her eggs in the water. But for other species, the hijinks continue. A female damselfly generally deposits her eggs in submerged plant tissue, so, still attached via the neck to her mate, she backs down a reed or other vegetation until she's completely covered by water. The silvery film of air coating her body supplies oxygen while she makes a slit in the plant and lays her eggs. Breaking out of the water's surface film is a challenge, but the male helps to pull her free. In some species, however, both male and female submerge and then labor to release first him and then her.

Their eggs hatch into carnivorous nymphs called naiads. A dragonfly naiad has a monstrously long lower jaw that abruptly reaches out to seize prey with a pair of claws at its tip. The naiad flees its own predators by squirting water from its anus. An inch-long insect can launch itself over twelve inches using this form of jet propulsion. Damselflies, which even as naiads are less coarse than the dragons, eschew the propulsion ability in favor of three feathery gills located at the end of their abdomens, which they wave about to get oxygen and also use like rudders.

Whether swimming naiads or winged adults, these creatures are voracious eaters of mosquitoes and other insects. The lifestyle has served them well. Once upon a time, even before the age of the dinosaurs, dragonflies patrolled swamps. Having survived over three hundred million years, the dragons and damsels continue to live happily ever after.

dragonfly naiad
seizing a tadpole

Skunk Cabbage

Latin name: *Lysichiton americanus*

Description: Large green leaves to 3 feet long; fleshy spike covered with small greenish yellow flowers, loosely encircled by a bright yellow hood.

Habitat: Bogs, marshes, wooded wetlands, wet meadows, mucky places.

ust when it seems the winter-wet weather will never cease, these cheery, neon-yellow plants come yoo-hooing up from the muck to announce the beginning of the end of the rainy season. I'm always so glad to see skunk cabbage, I couldn't care less what it smells like.

But, really, its odor is not that bad. This Northwest native species' reputation is sullied by that of its obnoxious purple-tinged eastern relative. Although you wouldn't want to use our skunk cabbage in a spring floral arrangement, it doesn't give off the same rotting-flesh smell that its eastern cousin does. The western version definitely exudes a musky odor, but you'd have to bruise the leaves before you smell some serious skunkiness.

Our versatile skunk cabbage attracts both bees, who like sweet scents, and beetles, who follow stench. These insects inadvertently pollinate the plant as they gather food. The plant releases different odors at different temperatures, enticing the pollinator most likely to be active.

Regardless of its smell, black bears eat the leaves, flowers, and especially the roots of skunk cabbage. Their enthusiasm for the plant has long been noted and gave rise to inaccurate folklore concerning the bear's intestinal requirements. In 1597 the English herbalist John Gerard wrote about the European skunk cabbage, called cuckoopint:

> Beares after they haue lien in their dens forty dayes without any manner of sustenance, but what they get with licking and sucking their owne feet, do as soone as they come forth eate the herbe Cuckowpint, through the windie nature whereof the hungry gut is opened and made fit againe to receiue sustenance: for by abstaining from food so long a time, the gut is shrunke or drawne so close together, that in a manner it is quite shut up. . . .

As much as I enjoy the image of newly awakened, gassy bears wandering the woods, it is folklore rather than fact.

Unlike bears, people can eat the hot, peppery root only after careful preparation. Skunk cabbage leaves and roots contain microscopic needle-like calcium oxalate crystals, which are severely irritating: they cause the throat and tongue to swell and can restrict breathing. Northwestern Native American tribes roasted or dried the roots, which destroyed the crystals and rid the plant of its peppery taste. The root was a welcome (although not a favorite) food after a sparse winter. The leaves were extremely useful for holding, covering, and storing food items such as berries and bulbs. They conveniently continue to grow after the flowering parts have died, and in shady areas often reach three feet long and one foot wide—the largest of any Northwest native plant.

It's the leaves' resemblance to garden cabbage, rather than any family relationship, that gave the plant its common name. But it was the cheery canary-yellow hood, sheltering the stalk with its tiny flowers, that earned the plant its genus name *Lysichiton* (loose tunic). A close look at one of the protected flowers in early spring reveals four pinhead powder puffs full of bright yellow powder—the pollen awaiting arrival of the bee or beetle. The stalk quickly outgrows its hood, and after the flowers are pollinated, berry-like fruits appear embedded along the stalk. The greenish to red fruits each contain one or two seeds. By midsummer only the huge green leaves will be left standing.

A wonderful Klamath Indian legend explains the plant's spike and hood. Before the salmon arrived, skunk cabbage fed the people and kept them from starvation. When the first fish finally swam upriver, skunk cabbage hailed them and explained his role. In reward, salmon gave skunk cabbage an elk-skin blanket and a war club. He still stands beside the rivers, wearing the blanket (hood) and holding the war club (stalk).

I like that legend because it treats with nobility the plant that once kept generations alive during lean times—the same plant that nowadays offers the first golden glimmer of sunnier days to come.

Common Horsetail

Latin name: *Equisetum arvense*

Description: To 18 inches tall; hollow, jointed, tubular stems, delicately ribbed; wiry green branches in whorls at joints; light green overall.

Habitat: Alongside ponds, streams, ditches, wooded wetlands, and seeps; can thrive on railway and road embankments if underground stems are in wet soil.

Although horsetails have been around for three hundred million years, their glory days were about seventy-five million years ago, when tree-sized versions lifted their heads high. Along with their relations the giant ferns and club mosses, ancient horsetail ancestors became the great coal-forming plants of prehistory. The resulting "soft" (or "cannel") coal burns with a particularly bright flame.

Though much smaller, today's descendants of those high-flying horsetails aren't doing so badly these days either. The common, or field, horsetail has been called one of the ten most common plant species in the world.

These primitive plants don't ask for much. Sunshine, access to water, and soil (even sandy or clayey soil) provide everything they need. Horsetails lack flowers and fruits, so they don't rely on insects or birds to help propagate their species. Their reproductive strategy

SPORE

DRY
ELATORS

WET

is similar to that of their ancient kin, ferns and club mosses.

In early spring, horsetail's underground roots send up its first tender stems. These pale, buff-colored fronds cannot photosynthesize. They grow perhaps six inches high and are tipped with a cone-shaped head covered with close-fitting scales.

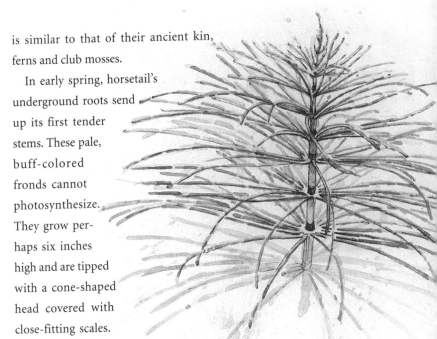

Underneath the scales are one-celled spores, which can be considered analogous to seeds in less-primitive plants. When the scales open at maturity, the globe-shaped spores are released. This takes only a few weeks, and the stems then turn brownish and wither.

Each spore has four appendages shaped something like straps, called electors. The electors wrap around the spore in a spiral when wet and uncoil when dry, and this movement helps disperse the spores and propel them through the soil. The spores eventually develop into minute male or female plants called *prothalli*, which produce either sperm or eggs. Moisture allows the sperm to swim to an egg, which, once fertilized, develops into a new plant. Covering their bets, horsetail can also spread vegetatively from below-ground rootstocks.

By the time those buff-colored fertile fronds have dropped their load of spores, the light-green sterile shoots have begun to emerge. These are the familiar plants shaped like bottle brushes. They arise from the same rootstock as the spore-bearing stems, and their job is to photosynthesize. They will continue to live and produce food until fall.

Different species of horsetail vary in the habitats they prefer. But the common horsetail gained its name by being the one we most frequently encounter. Some people call horsetails "scouring rushes," but others reserve this term for a similar plant, E. hyemale, which has no branches and is banded with light and dark rings. Both scouring rushes and horsetails have long been used to polish hard woods and clean cooking vessels. This useful characteristic is a result of silica crystals embedded in their tissues. (Silica is a hard mineral found in quartz and glass. I've heard that if you pluck a horsetail stem and carefully hold a lit match below it, the silica will transform itself into tiny beads of glass—but I've never been able to perform this magic.)

Despite the tiny bits of silica, Northwest Indians ate horsetails; the early green shoots were especially welcome after a long winter without many fresh vegetables, and the rootstocks and the conelike tops of certain species were also eaten. Horsetails are a food you can eat for dinner—and then use to clean the cooking pot.

Water Strider

Latin name: *Gerris remigis*

Description: About ¹/₂ to ⁵/₈ inch long; thin body, most likely wingless; six long, slender legs.

Habitat: Ponds, lakes, brooks, slow-moving streams.

Water striders thrive on tension—water tension, that is. The tendency of water's molecules to stick together and the insects' special adaptations make it possible for striders to live on the fine line between water and air.

Gazing at a pond or a slow-moving stream on a sunny day, you may notice the common water strider's shadow before you spot the slender, dark insect suspended above it. There are hundreds of species of striders, some of which prefer fast streams or even open ocean. The most common species in the Northwest (and throughout North America) is *Gerris remigis*.

Striders have three pairs of legs, but only the back two pairs are immediately obvious. These long, thin legs sprawl over the water and help to distribute the small animal's weight. The middle legs act as oars, rowing the insect over the water, while the hindmost pair are twin rudders used for steering.

Looking at the strider's shadow, you may notice what appear to be pads where the legs contact the water. These shadows are created by the dimple each leg makes on the water surface. The delicate weight of the strider causes the elastic water surface to bend a bit, just as a person walking on a trampoline makes depressions without breaking through the fabric.

The tips of the water strider's legs are coated with oily, waterproof hairs, which help to evenly distribute the animal's weight. In fact, the whole lower portion of a water strider's body is coated with these fine hairs, which also repel water and trap air. Should the insect inadvertently break the water tension and plunge beneath the surface, the air trapped in the hairs will help it resurface. Striders keep these hairs clean by grooming them with their front legs, much like a cat does.

The insects' small front legs are easy to overlook, but they are used in the important business of capturing food. Striders prowl the pond eating living and dead insects and crustaceans on the water surface. These may have floated up from below or may have fallen in and are struggling or drowned. The strider nabs the prey with its front legs and pierces its shell (or exoskeleton) with a needlelike mouthpart. Juices pumped into the prey stun it and dissolve its internal body parts. The strider then sucks out the victim's liquefied insides. The surface tension of water plays an important role during the hunt: sensory organs in the insect's legs alert it to tiny ripples and help guide it to a struggling lunch.

At least some species of striders also create their own ripple patterns for use in mating. In spring and early summer, males select a territory near a plant stem or some other material suitable for egg-laying. They then send out small ripple signals: one pattern communicates a male's desire for a mate, and the other apparently warns off other males. If a female is interested, she grasps the stem or other object as the male mounts her. She lays her eggs while the male stands guard, sending threatening ripples to other males and attacking them if they venture too close.

Their nymphs hatch in a couple of weeks, break through the water tension from below, and climb onto its surface. They molt several times, growing larger each time, and after a month or so are ready to mate. Water striders generally have two broods per year, and the adults of the second generation spend the winter ashore near the water. They hibernate under leaves, rocks, logs, or other vegetation until the change in season indicates it's time to resume a life of tension on the water.

Bullfrog

Latin name: *Rana catesbeiana*

Description: To 8 inches long; yellowish green to dark brown, sometimes mottled; smooth skin; large, round ear membrane is same size as eye or slightly smaller in females, and much larger than eye in males.

Habitat: In or near permanent water, including ponds, lakes, slow rivers, reservoirs, marshes, and irrigation ditches with vegetation.

It must have seemed like a good idea at the time. Why not transport bullfrogs from the Eastern and Midwestern states to the Pacific Northwest and release them? Bullfrogs can be fun to catch, and their legs are good eating—and the watery Northwest would be a welcoming habitat for them.

A little too welcoming, as it has turned out. The bullfrog has few predators here, and because it is considerably larger than the Northwest's native frogs, it not only outcompetes them for territory and food but eats them as well. Where bullfrogs thrive, you're unlikely to find any other frog. The big frog is also implicated in the precipitous decline of native western pond turtles.

Bullfrogs were introduced here by various groups, including Depression-era frog farmers, who raised them for their meaty legs, and state wildlife agencies, which released them as a new game animal in the 1920s or '30s (bullfrogs are still subject to game regulations). Whatever their original source, bullfrogs are now widespread in the Northwest.

In addition to native frogs and young turtles, the voracious bullfrog will eat anything it can fit its huge mouth around, including worms, insects, fish, young snakes, and crayfish. The largest specimens even swallow ducklings, other small birds, and small mammals such as mice. The bullfrog, like other frogs, lacks chewing teeth and swallows its prey whole. To manage a large meal, it uses both forelegs to cram the entire creature into its mouth at once. The frog even pulls its bulging eyes down into their sockets (just as it does when it blinks) and uses them to help stuff the food down its throat.

During its mating season of May through August, the male bullfrog lays claim to a small stretch of water and the real estate bordering it. He solicits females and warns off other males with a deep "jug-o-rum" call. Experiments have shown that the round ear membranes on either side of the bullfrog's head resonate and amplify the call. How the frog manages to use his eardrums in such a way without deafening himself is still a mystery.

Should another male arrive in his territory to challenge him, the two engage in a wrestling match. They lunge up out of the shallows, using their forelegs to grab or shove one another. The weaker one gets dunked, and the baddest bullfrog gets the disputed territory. He also gets the females, who judge his territory by its egg-laying sites. If she likes what she sees, a female swims up to the proprietor. He promptly seizes her from behind with his front legs, and the two drift around until she lays her eggs; as she does, he adds his sperm.

Bullfrogs are exceedingly prolific. The couple's large raft of five thousand to over fifteen thousand eggs floats on the water's surface for four or five days and sinks just before the eggs hatch. The resulting tadpoles are larger than those of any native frog and will take a relatively leisurely two years to metamorphose. Even as a juvenile, the bullfrog is as large as the native adults; any frog you see in the Northwest that is more than four or five inches long is apt to be a bullfrog.

Bullfrogs are the starlings of Pacific Northwest pond life. Like that introduced bird, they are a pleasant part of their original habitat, where they maintain a naturally balanced population. Outside their indigenous range, both are obnoxious. Bullfrogs, the amphibious starling, are loud, pushy, fecund, widespread, and here to stay.

Yellow Pond-Lily

Latin name: *Nuphar polysepalum*

Description: Bright yellow flowers 1½ to 3 inches in diameter bloom June to mid-August; heart-shaped flat leaves grow to 12 inches; flowers and leaves float on the water, or rise slightly above it.

Habitat: Shallow lakes, ponds, marshes, slow-moving streams.

One of my favorite trails leads to a lake filled with yellow pond-lilies, their flowers arranged like so many floating teacups. The shiny leaves lie flat like saucers, usually with edges slightly upturned. Each summer the pond reminds me of a soggy tea party set for dragonflies, muskrats, and frogs.

It's not just my imagination: pond-lilies offer a banquet to a variety of insects and animals. Lift any one of those shiny saucer-leaves and you're likely to find insect eggs attached underneath. Some of these, upon hatching, will feast on the leaves that sheltered them. And ducks eat the plants' seeds, beavers dive to retrieve the rootstocks, muskrats dine on most parts of the plant, and deer wade into the shallows to nibble leaves, flowers, and stems.

Most land plants have breathing pores, called *stomata*, on the undersides of their leaves. This design is obviously not workable for the pond-lily, though: its microscopic stomata are found on the top sides of its leaves. The shiny, waxy surface of the leaves readily sheds any errant water droplets.

Many insects seek protection under the sheltering leaves—which also make convenient rafts for frogs and landing pads for dragonflies. Despite all this use and activity, the pond-lily's sole purpose is to make more pond-lilies. It does this by enticing beetles and flies with its pollen. In the center of the flower is a knoblike projection that includes its reproductive organs. A new flower at first opens only slightly, and a visiting beetle must rub against the male organs, thereby inadvertently collecting sticky pollen. This will be delivered to the female organs of other plants as the beetle continues to make its rounds gathering food—so it can fulfill *its* purpose of creating more beetles.

After fertilization, oval seedpods develop, which eventually rupture so the seeds can sink to the pond bottom and take root. Later these seeds will send their own flower and leaf buds reaching up to unfurl in the light and air. A long stem is attached to the notch of each heart-shaped leaf, anchoring it to the plant's roots in the muck below. The plant is also able to launch new leaves and flowers via spreading rootstocks at the pond's bottom.

The pond-lily's seedpods were an extremely important food to some Native American tribes, especially the Klamath, who call the plant *wokas*. Ceremony and dancing surrounded the ripening of the seedpods. When shamans determined the time was right, the women spent days gathering pods from dugout canoes. Seeds were ground into flour or meal, dried for later use, or popped like popcorn.

The massive rootstocks also had many medicinal uses. The roots were heated and pressed against rheumatic joints or applied for chest pain. Different tribes used the plant to treat various illnesses, including tuberculosis, ulcers, heart conditions, asthma, and cancer. Some of these medicinal applications are still in use today.

You might occasionally see white or pink-tinged pond-lilies. These fragrant plants are immigrants from eastern states and are much less common that the yellow Northwest native. Another native plant that looks similar to pond-lilies is the watershield (*Brasenia schreberi*). The leaves of this plant are oval, lacking the notch that makes pond-lily leaves heart-shaped. Another way to distinguish watershield is that the undersides of its leaves and its rootstock are covered with a thick, shiny, gelatinous coating.

When a trail leads you to a pond whose gleaming surface is set with yellow pond-lily teacups, you might consider finding a log or some other convenient dry seat and taking your place. You never know who else, of the many insects and animals acquainted with pond-lily, might also accept the invitation.

Caddisfly

Latin name: Order Trichoptera; various genera and species

Description: Larvae caterpillar-like, up to 1⅛ inches long; adults up to 1 inch long, dull-colored, four-winged, and mothlike.

Habitat: Streams and rivers, lakes, ponds, marshes; larvae on, among, or under rocks, pebbles, or sand; different species prefer specific types of water and kinds of bottoms.

Standing beside a stream one summer day, I watched an American dipper procuring late-afternoon snacks. The sooty-gray bird would stick its head underwater and emerge with something dangling from its bill. The treat seemed to require a few sharp shakes of the bird's head before being swallowed. After the dipper moved downstream, I checked to see what it had been after. Strewn among the rocks of the stream bottom were the little stony cases of caddisfly larvae.

The larvae, often called caddisworms, look something like caterpillars—but unless you're a dipper you're unlikely to see the naked creature. Many kinds of caddisworms create their own protective cases, which they enlarge as they molt and grow. Depending on species, these might be made out of sand, tiny pebbles, bits of sticks and plant material, or tiny snail shells. They are held together with an adhesive silk, and are constructed in different shapes, such as cylinders, elongated cones, spiraling twists, or tiny turtle shells. The cases are so distinctive that species can be identified by the type of homes they build.

The caddisworm secures itself inside its home with a pair of stout hooks toward the end of its abdomen. The dipper I'd been watching had clamped its bill onto the front bit of the animal, and then jerked the rest of it out of the case with quick shakes before being able to swallow it. Caddisworms are also an important food for freshwater fish such as trout, who reportedly try to suck them out of their cases but are willing to eat the entire thing if need be.

Not all caddisworms hide in cases, however. Some species spin underwater silken nets that, like spiders' webs, catch food. This type of caddisfly larva, considered more primitive than the portable-house-building type, is found in rushing water. It makes a trap, perhaps one inch across by a half-inch high, from silk spun from its lower lip. Again, different species make webs of different shapes, which have descriptive names such as trumpet net or finger net. The animal generally lies in wait near its web, and perhaps partially hidden by it, until some unsuspecting minute critter is swept into the trap. The little carnivore pounces upon the prey and devours it. Still other types of caddisworms make do without either web or case, and simply creep over rocks in search of food. These larvae may be carnivores or vegetarians content with plant matter.

Eventually, after a year or more and several molts, the larva is ready to leave the stream and take to the air as a winged caddisfly. All types pupate beneath the water; the case-making type seal themselves into their homes for their final molt. The emerging fly must make its way to the surface, and some types use their old molted skins as a convenient launching pad from which to take off.

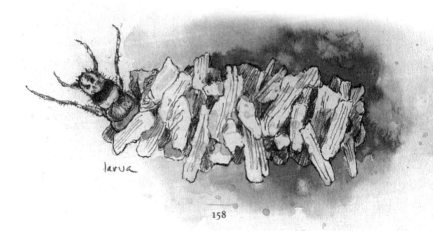

larva

I'm much better acquainted with caddisfly larvae than with their adult forms, though it's likely I've encountered many more adults. These fly at night and are commonly attracted to outside lights. No doubt I've mistaken many for moths. There are basic and discernible differences between moths and caddisflies, however. The most obvious of these are the antennae. Caddisflies have very long, slender antennae, while moths have shorter ones that are at least somewhat feathered. Moths are also covered with tiny scales, while caddisflies have minute hairs on their wings. And moths have a coiled, tonguelike proboscis, which caddisflies lack, since they rarely eat during the brief time they are in their adult forms.

adult

Caddisflies mate in flight, over water, and the male dies shortly thereafter. The female lays her eggs in the water or on overhanging vegetation, from which the young drop into the water upon hatching. She does not live long after completing her motherly duties. The caddisfly larvae that eventually spin webs or create clever homes will become not only treats for various birds and fish but also interesting finds for curious people who peer into ponds and streams.

Signal Crayfish

Latin name: *Pacifastacus leniusculus*

Description: To 7 inches from head to tail but usually under 5 inches; two pair of antennae; first pair of legs end in pincers, four pairs of walking legs; can be black, brown, reddish, gray, or bluish, depending on habitat.

Habitat: Ponds, lakes, and streams, often under rocks or in crevices.

Crawdad, crawfish, mudbug—we have almost as many names as we do uses for crayfish. These miniature lobster look-alikes are used in classroom dissections and laboratory research, as aquarium pets, as bait, and as a culinary treat.

Because the Pacific Northwest's native species, the signal crayfish, is relatively large and has tasty meat, it has been widely introduced outside of its natural distribution. Unfortunately, just as introduced species such as bullfrogs and starlings are pushing out the native species in the Northwest, the signal crayfish has outcompeted local crayfish species in California and in Europe, causing population declines and perhaps extinctions.

In the Northwest, prey and predator have evolved along with the signal crayfish, and it is simply a part of the aquatic food web. Its prey includes small animals such as algae, snails, worms, and tadpoles, and small plants. Predators include otters, raccoons, mink, turtles, snakes, some fish, birds, and humans.

The crayfish has effective defenses against its many enemies. The pincers of even a small specimen are strong enough to break human skin. The little crustacean can also make a quick getaway. The crayfish contracts its abdominal muscles and fans its tail to shoot backward with surprising speed.

In late summer and early fall, males are on the lookout for females. Finding one, a male seizes her, rolls her over, and releases sperm on the underside of her tail. This isn't immediately washed away by the water because the sperm attach to the tail with slender white strings (which people sometimes mistake for worms). When the female releases her eggs onto the waiting sperm, they are fertilized. A secreted sticky substance holds the developing eggs against the underside of the female's body. Because the eggs, which can number several hundred, somewhat resemble berries, the female is said to be "in berry."

The female carries her eggs all winter, and by the time they hatch in spring each will have formed an attachment cord called a telson thread. The tiny hatchlings remain secured to their mother via these threads and by clinging to whatever part of her they can grab with their miniature claws. Their first molt breaks the telson threads, but the young cling to their mother with their pincers for perhaps another ten days before they release their grip and try their own luck at nabbing food and eluding enemies.

Like other hard-bodied relations, such as shrimp and lobsters, the crayfish will molt many times in its first year and will continue to molt, though less often, throughout its life. When it molts, the crayfish's hard outer covering, called an exoskeleton, splits down the back. Already sporting a fresh, soft-skinned covering, the animal pulls itself out of the old skin and then pumps in water to expand so that when its new exoskeleton hardens, there will be room inside to grow. During the soft-shell stage, the crustacean is particularly vulnerable to predation, but an advantage of molting is that the crayfish is able to begin regenerating lost legs, claws, or antennae.

Crayfish have two pairs of antennae and both pairs are used to touch, taste, and smell. The longer pair senses what's going on a little distance ahead of and behind the animal. The smaller set, called antennules, attend to things close-in. Both pairs, as well as the claws, are covered with tiny hairs that help the animal sense its surroundings.

These animals are extremely sensitive to water quality. Although scientific understanding of which pollutants affect crayfish is hazy, it is known that the little crustaceans will die or move elsewhere when the oxygen level of the water decreases. In addition to all their other uses and attributes, crayfish are also an excellent indicator of pollution. It's rather one-sided, however, to consider only the ways in which nonhumans can serve *us*. To be fair, we could contemplate the uses that these animals might have for humans—and conclude that we make dandy transportation devices to places the signal crayfish would not otherwise be able to colonize. Other than that clever quality, as far as crayfish are concerned, humans are probably worthless.

Red-Winged Blackbird

Latin name: *Agelaius phoeniceus*

Description: 8 inches; male glossy black except for bright red shoulder patches lined with yellow at lower edge; female dark brown above, streaked brown on white background below.

Habitat: Marshes, ponds, streamsides, roadside ditches; also farmlands and fields outside of breeding season.

I f you follow the burbling flow of a red-winged blackbird's song it will lead you, appropriately, to water. The liquid calls of these birds and the flashing of their brilliant shoulder patches divide a wetland into fiercely defended territories.

Although some of these birds may remain in the Northwest year-round, most winter in warmer climes, as far south as Costa Rica. Many birders and other people recognize the arrival of spring with the appearance of red-winged blackbirds in local ponds and roadside ditches. The older males arrive first, females (who in their camouflage coloration look more like large sparrows than blackbirds) follow some weeks later, and first-year males make up the last wave.

The first-come males vie for good nesting sites. When a bird has claimed a place, he fluffs his feathers to reveal the crimson shoulder badges, proclaiming himself the law of the land and ready to attack any who dares confront him. For this reason, a bird still looking for a territory will usually travel under cover, with his own epaulets hidden under black feathers. By doing so, he signals his intent to leave peaceably if confronted by the rightful owner. Challengers arrive with epaulets blazing, sending a message that cannot be ignored.

The males are so concerned about their property rights that they even run off newly arriving females. But the females are persistent. They judge a male by the quality of nesting sites in his territory, and once a female has identified a mate, she lurks about his property until he figures out why she is there.

For many years it's been known that male red-winged blackbirds are monogamous if there are enough of them to go around but polygamous if there are fewer males than females. A male may have as many as fifteen mates (though the number is usually fewer than that), all nesting within his territory. But a more recent study has revealed that many of the females do a little trysting on the sly—DNA testing proved the young in their nests had different daddies. In most of these cases, the fathers were the territorial male and a neighboring one.

Like most birds, blackbirds mate with a "cloacal kiss." (The cloaca is the anal opening through which both the reproductive and excretory systems discharge.) The male mounts the female, and both move their tails aside to briefly press together their cloacas for the passage of sperm.

The female builds a nest, usually attached to cattails or other vegetation, and she has sole responsibility for incubating her three or four eggs. The male, meanwhile, continues an exuberant defense of his territory. Individual males have been seen to drive larger predatory birds into the water and to ride the back of a crow, furiously pecking away as the crow made its escape.

The young fledge in just eleven to fourteen days, and the female often produces a second brood and occasionally a third. Many (perhaps half) of the young are lost to predators including other birds, foxes, weasels, and mink.

By their second year, the young males will be ready to claim territories of their own, belting out their springtime serenade. Various attempts to render that trickling lyric into English syllables include "o-ka-leee," "kong-ka-REE," "pull-the-LE-ver," etc. But my favorite attempt suggests Elmer Fudd calling for the demise of his nemesis Bugs Bunny: "Kill the WAAAA-bit!"

River Otter

Latin name: *Lutra canadensis*

Description: To 50 inches long, including tail; fur dark brown on back, lighter on undersides; hind legs slightly longer than front legs so body is slightly tilted; webbed feet; thick, tapering tail.

Habitat: Areas with fresh, brackish, or salt water: lakes, streams, rivers, marshes, estuaries, and seashores.

River otters know how to have a good time. Human observers, even those not prone to frivolity, use words like "frolic" and "cavort" to describe the animals' antics. Only the most staid of scientists or nature writers, in dread fear of anthropomorphizing, insist that the animals' mud-sliding and snow-tobogganing are simply modes of transportation. Pah! Otters play.

Unfortunately, seeing otters frolicking and cavorting in the wild has become something of a rarity. They've been trapped for fur and occasionally killed by anglers who begrudge them fish, but the massive extermination of beavers in the late 1800s may have been the greatest factor in the reduction of otter populations. The beavers provided lots of ponds and other wetland habitat—and otters depend on water. Water pollution and pesticide poisoning may have also hurt the otter population, both by killing fish prey outright and by the concentration of poisons in fish.

Still, it's certainly possible to see river otters in the wild, especially if you happen spend a lot of time near water (perhaps wearing waders and with a fishing pole in your hand) or if you know something about the animals' habits and signs. A slide, for example, is a slicked-down furrow on a bank, perhaps eight inches wide, leading into the water. Otters mark their territory with black scat (feces), usually deposited in a repeatedly used, prominent place just out of the water. Near the water's edge, perhaps under bushes, you might also spot rolling places. These spots are about three feet in diameter and are often in a sandy area, or may show dirt where vegetation has been rubbed away. Here the wet animals vigorously roll around, possibly as a way of drying or cleaning and grooming their fur.

In places near human habitation, otters are primarily nocturnal; in less-developed areas, they are active from daybreak to midmorning and again in evening hours. Because they don't hibernate, otters are active throughout the year. Where streams join rivers, the additional nutrients result in more prey, which may result in a greater chance of seeing otters.

A staple of the otter's diet is fish, most often nongame species like minnows, suckers, or sticklebacks, though they also eat small trout and bass. Depending on the season, they also snack on crayfish, frogs, salamanders, some small mammals and birds, berries, and other foods.

During the winter months, a male otter's thoughts turn to female otters and he may travel long distances overland to find one. A female, meanwhile, may leave scent marks within her territory to help lead him in the right direction. Having successfully found one another, the pair mates in the water, perhaps repeating the performance several times over a couple of days. Like other members of the weasel family, otters have delayed implantation of fertilized eggs: the eggs do not attach to the uterus, or begin to develop, for nine or ten months. But once the eggs are implanted, the resulting pups are born only seven weeks later. Before their birth, the mother has prepared a den for them. She doesn't dig her own burrow, but will renovate the underground home of a muskrat or beaver, or find space in a hollow log or among tree roots. In the Northwest, a litter usually consists of two or three pups.

At about ten or twelve weeks old, the mother introduces the young to water. The pups often resist getting better acquainted, and the mother may drag a baby in by the scruff of its neck. Or she may let a pup ride on her back as she swims, and then suddenly dive. For a species that is so connected to water and that shows such agility when older, the young have a surprisingly difficult time getting comfortable in their liquid environment. They seem head-heavy, and sputter and snort until they get the hang of swimming.

In his fascinating book *Mammals of the Pacific Northwest: From the Coast to the High Cascades*, Chris Maser reports that, when traveling on land, mothers rebuke wayward young by nipping their noses. The chastised youngster stops and lies still on the ground. As if it were truly remorseful, a strongly punished pup will lie on its back and will not move forward until "the mother returns and caresses it."

The young probably stay with their mother for about eight months, until midwinter, when they disperse. Once on their own territories, they establish new rolling places and prominent spots to leave their mark. They may create slides, or seek rapids in which to body-surf. Otters, unconcerned by any debate about the motives behind their antics, know how to have a good time.

Muskrat

Latin name: *Ondatra zibethicus*

Description: 15 to 24 inches long, including vertically flattened tail, which is nearly half the length of body; dark brown glossy fur on back, sides can be reddish brown, throat light gray, appearing nearly white; small eyes and ears.

Habitat: Ponds, marshes, and other wetlands; slow-moving rivers and streams.

The muskrat is one of those animals whose name fits it rather nicely. While not really a rat, it *is* a rodent, and it does have musk glands. This pair of glands, located at the animal's rear end, secrete a yellow substance that is musky and somewhat sweet-smelling. The secretions are exuded especially during mating season and probably serve to mark territory.

Although a mating pair may get together any time from May through October, muskrat love is nothing to sing about. After copulation, the two go their separate ways without a backward glance. The female births up to eleven young, usually mates again while she is nursing, and has two or three litters annually.

East of the Cascades, muskrats frequently build vegetative houses that rise up out of the water, but on the west side, they seem to prefer underground burrows. They access these by underwater openings that angle up into dry-chambered interiors. Animals on both sides of the mountains sometimes build rafts from vegetation, which they climb aboard to enjoy a floating meal. Muskrats eat cattails, rushes, skunk-cabbage, ferns, and other soft plants. They also sometimes take small animals like crayfish, turtles, snails, and tadpoles.

The muskrat is well adapted to its aquatic life. It can dive for fifteen minutes at a time, and its mouth can seal shut behind the two front teeth while the animal clips off underwater plants. Slightly webbed toes and stiff hairs fringing the back feet help move the muskrat through the water, while its long tail acts as a rudder.

If you see a muskrat swimming, or from a distance, you might well confuse it with two other animals found in or near water, beaver and nutria. Size is the key in the first instance: the body of the largest muskrat would be less than half the size of the smallest beaver.

In some places, a nutria might be more likely to be confused with a muskrat, though again, the former is a larger animal. Nutria, originally from South America, were imported for use on fur farms in the 1940s. When the promised profits didn't materialize, enough of the creatures were set free to form feral populations in some areas (such as Oregon's Willamette Valley, where they have multiplied to pest proportions). The nutria is one of those animals whose name does *not* fit particularly well. Not only does it sound more like a refreshing new sports drink than an animal, but it could confuse people who know that *nutria* is Spanish for "otter." For this reason, some prominent biologists recommend switching to the alternative name of "coypu," from the nutria's scientific name, *Myocastor coypus.*

Identifying any of the furry water-loving rodents is easiest if the animal in question cooperates and presents its tail. Beavers, of course, have the well-known paddle-shaped tail; nutria/coypu have a long, rounded tail; muskrats have a long, vertically flattened tail.

The two natives, beaver and muskrat, have similar habitats but have evolved in ways that lessen competition. Nutria, on the other hand, are in direct competition with muskrats and tend to muscle them out of their home turf. It is not the meek, unfortunately, who will inherit the wetlands.

Beaver

Latin name: *Castor canadensis*

Description: To 4 feet long, including tail up to 18 inches; dark brown fur; tail flat, scaly, and hairless; small eyes and ears; webbed hind feet; orange front teeth.

Habitat: Streams, rivers, ponds, lakes, and marshes.

Historians would agree that a large rodent led the way to Western expansion of the United States and Canada. In the waning years of the 1700s and the first half of the 1800s, the pursuit of valuable beaver pelts pushed much of the exploration and early settlement of unknown western territory. For several decades, the pelts were the continent's most valuable export to Europe. In addition to use in fur coats, robes, and trimmings, the underfur of beavers was pounded into a superior felt used in gentlemen's hats; that fad lasted until beaver became scarce and silk hats came into vogue.

Dead beavers may have provided the impetus for exploration, but living beavers shaped the land itself. North America's largest living rodent was once so numerous that virtually every pond, stream, river, or other suitable waterway hosted at least one colony. Through their impressive engineering skills, beavers transformed dry land into ponds, flooding out some species and creating habitat for numerous others. Eventually, when the ponds filled with silt trapped by their dams, the animals moved on, leaving behind meadows and fertile soil.

Although their numbers are now sorely diminished, a newly established beaver colony still has an awesome impact on the land. As their population rebounds, this increasingly brings them into conflict with humans who have already claimed the area.

Beavers are driven to create wetlands as a safe haven for themselves and their families. On land, they are slow, rather ponderous creatures that could make a fine meal for large predators like bears or mountain lions. Their young are vulnerable to a range of predators from great horned owls to coyotes. But in the water, adults are safe, and, with the exception of attacks by otters, their young are as well. No wonder beavers are genetically programmed to react at the sound of escaping water and plug up the leak.

Beavers are vegetarians, and everyone knows they eat trees. Fewer people realize it is the thin, growing, inner layer of bark of mostly deciduous trees that the animal feeds on, along with leaves, twigs, and buds. The skinned limbs and logs are then used for building and repairs. A beaver's diet also includes skunk cabbage, some berries and ferns, fungi, pond-lilies, and algae. During the fall, beavers are eager to store food for the coming cold winter. They stick branches into the muck at the bottom of their pond, where the wood keeps nicely and is accessible even if the pond freezes over.

It's often assumed that beavers deliberately cut a tree so that it falls into the water, but it's really just a matter of luck. When a tree falls the wrong way, the beavers can sometimes shove it into the water anyway. But around a beaver pond, it's possible to find felled trees that proved unmovable, toppled ones that are hung up in another tree's branches, and big trunks that were gnawed only partway through before the beaver realized it had bitten off more than it could chew.

Several adaptations aid the beaver's aquatic lifestyle. Valves close off the animal's ears and nose when it dives. Transparent membranes, similar to eyelids, protect the beaver's eyes from floating debris. Lung capacity and economical use of air allow it to remain submerged for fifteen minutes. Skin flaps that seal behind the front teeth let the animal carry branches in its mouth. And special glands near the reproductive opening of their bodies exude a waterproofing oil, which the beaver transfers to its fur with its forepaws.

Beavers are thought to mate for life, and the couple shares its lodge with not only the current year's three or four kits but also the surviving young from the previous year. The extended family's home can be the classic dome planted out in the middle of the water, a similar aboveground home on the bank, or an underground burrow in the side of the bank. In all cases, the inner part of the home is high and dry above the waterline, while its access tunnel is located underwater.

Beavers are often cited as second only to humans in their ability to transform habitat. If you want to erect a skyscraper or pour yet another asphalt parking lot, hire a human engineer. But if you'd prefer to transform a stream into a pond or reclaim a wetland, leave it to beavers.

Great Blue Heron

Latin name: *Ardea herodias*

Description: 3 or more feet; bluish gray body; long bill, neck, and legs;
long black plumes extend from head.

Habitat: Salt or fresh water, in tideflats, ponds, streams, or lakeside, but also in fields
some distance from water or near backyard pools.

A hunting great blue heron seems outfitted with only two speeds: slow motion and fast forward. This large bird may stand knee-deep in ponds and rivers, staring intently at the water for long, patient minutes. Or it may wade slowly, drawing one foot from the water and placing it precisely back in, toes closed to a point to avoid creating any warning ripples.

But when a frog or fish cruises into range, the heron suddenly slams into high gear. It makes a lightning jab into the water with its bill, seizes the animal, and swallows it head first and whole. Small fish make up the bulk of its diet, but the heron also nabs crayfish, dragonflies, and insect larvae, and uses its bill to stab larger fish. A heron hunting in a field or meadow is probably after insects and mice.

Native to the Pacific Northwest, the great blue heron has earned many names over time. The Nisqually tribe is said to call it "our grandfather," settlers often called it "big cranky" or "long john," and today birders refer to it by the initials "GBH."

The sight of a wading or flying blue heron is not unusual today, but in the early 1900s, the heron population was severely reduced due to a whim of fashion: the feathers of both herons and egrets adorned women's hats, and thousands of the birds were killed annually to feed the fad. An organization that would later become the National Audubon Society was launched by two prominent Boston women who opposed the slaughter. The public outcry they helped spur resulted in laws that protected these birds and spared the great blue from being wiped out by a fashion craze.

The heron has two ingenious ways to care for those once-coveted feathers. Like other water birds, it uses its bill to "paint" its feathers with a waterproofing oil gathered from a gland at the base of its tail, but an additional tactic helps keep them clean. The tips of special feathers on its breast, called powder down, disintegrate into a dust that the heron uses to clean itself. The fine, waxy powder absorbs fish oil and helps keep feathers water repellent. The bird also grooms by using a serrated section on its middle toe as a comb.

Great blue herons are solitary birds most of the year, but in late February and early March the males and females court with displays that include neck-stretching and the raising and lowering of feathers. Sometimes a pair will groom the feathers of each other's head, neck, and back. Most endearingly, they might grasp the tips of each other's bills and then, in unison, rock their heads back and forth. The birds gather in nesting areas called heronries, usually located near water in remote, secluded woods. (The city of Portland, Oregon, however, boasts two rookeries within its city limits, the larger one located on Ross Island in the Willamette River.) They haul branches up into tall trees to make platform nests or repair old ones. After the female lays three to five eggs, the parents take turns sitting on them. Herons probably nest in a large group to help protect their gangly, helpless young.

In the first few weeks after their offspring hatch, one parent stands guard while the other goes fishing, but as the young birds grow it takes both parents to keep up with their demanding appetites. The constant comings and goings of the adults and the raucous calls of their young make the heronry a noisy, bustling place.

When the young herons leave the nest (usually only two or three survive at this point), they must hunt for themselves. The art of two-speed fishing apparently takes some time to learn. Studies have shown that the young birds expend far more energy than adults do in getting a satisfying meal. But each misstep and every miscalculated attempt perfects a young bird's technique. Eventually they master the great blue heron's art of slow, dignified concentration and wicked, fast jabs.

Belted Kingfisher

Latin name: *Ceryle alcyon*

Description: 12 inches; large blue-gray head with ragged crest; compact body with white neck and underparts; blue-gray belt across breast; females have an additional ruddy band across belly and rufous flanks.

Habitat: Near water, fresh or salt: streams, ponds, ocean, estuaries.

If you want to see a kingfisher, look to water. It's estimated that these birds were once found patrolling every waterway, small or large, across the country. But the same old sad song of habitat loss and killing of creatures believed to be in competition with people led to a precipitous decline in kingfisher populations.

When you do find one of these birds, it will probably be fishing. The mainstay of a kingfisher's diet is small fish, up to five inches long, although they are known to take crayfish, frogs, newts, mice, butterflies, moths, and other small creatures. The kingfishers I've seen spend a lot of time on a perch—a branch, a pier, or a convenient utility wire—gazing intently at the water below. When a small fish swims by, the kingfisher dives headfirst into the water to claim it. (Later, the bird will upchuck a pellet composed of scales, bones, and other undigestible items.) A kingfisher will also peruse its fishing ground on the wing, hovering briefly over its next meal before plummeting to the water. It takes the still-wriggling prey to a perch and whacks it to death against a branch before swallowing it.

Fishermen once embarked on campaigns to kill the birds, but today kingfishers are protected by federal law. The birds themselves have never been wont to share their fishing rights either. They are intensely territorial and, should another kingfisher dare enter the area, the resident charges full tilt after the intruder, hollering its rattling alarm call, which has been likened to a New Year's Eve noisemaker. The mad dash continues until the marauding kingfisher crosses the boundary and is driven off.

It seems odd that such an excitable, apparently irritable little bird was given a scientific species name that derives from the Greek *halcyon* (which now means "calm and peaceful"). The connection is that the Greeks noted two weeks of calm seas during the kingfisher's breeding season. They thought the birds built their nests on the open water, and believed that the gods favored them with smooth seas.

It's understandable that the ancients thought these birds nested out at sea; even today you can search every tree in a kingfisher's territory and still not find its nest. That's because they raise their young in burrows underground. Kingfishers relax their No-Trespassers-Allowed policy for the weeks that it takes to create more kingfishers. Male and female take turns digging into a bank, usually near water. They loosen stones and dirt with their bills and push them out of the burrow with their feet. (Their two middle toes are fused together for most of their length, which helps accomplish this task.) The excavated tunnel usually extends three to seven feet into the bank, although tunnels as long as fifteen feet have been measured. Depending on the soil's composition, it takes the birds three days to three weeks to create their nesting site. The burrow ends in a chamber where five to eight eggs are laid. The male kingfisher takes his turns brooding the eggs, and both parents feed the young after they hatch—an increasingly demanding task as the many babies grow.

Once the young are big enough (and no doubt the parents tired enough), the adults coax them out of their burrow by perching nearby with food in beak. After the young are fledged, the parents teach them to fish by dropping dead fish into the water. As they graduate to fishing on their own, which takes about three weeks, the family's tolerance of one another wears thin. The young leave to find territories of their own to drive other kingfishers out of, and the parents return to their own solitary lives. The days after their parental duties are completed, rather than their breeding season, would appear to be the kingfisher's true halcyon days.

Mallard

Latin name: *Anas platyrhynchos*

Description: 25 inches. Male in breeding plumage: metallic green head and neck, thin white collar around neck, chestnut breast, dark gray back, yellow bill. Female: mottled brown, orange bill with black markings. Nonbreeding male looks similar to female but retains yellow bill. Both sexes have bright blue patch on wings.

Habitat: Shallow ponds, streams, marshes, occasionally on sheltered salt water, especially in winter.

Mallards are so common they are not usually given their due measure of appreciation by birders. Males wearing breeding plumage are handsome enough that they would probably be avidly sought if they weren't nearly as hackneyed as robins.

And they're not just the most frequently sighted duck in the Pacific Northwest; mallards can be found in any bit of shallow fresh water larger than a puddle throughout the rest of North America, and in Europe and Asia. They may well be the most abundant duck in the entire Northern Hemisphere.

This hardy, adaptable bird has had a long affiliation with people. Mallards were domesticated as early as the first century A.D. Today, all domesticated or barnyard ducks (except the Muscovy) can claim the mallard as ancestor. No other duck has been as useful or economically important to the human race.

Still, it's not as though the bird just lies down on a platter for us to eat. Hunters consider it a wily duck: during hunting season it is easily alarmed and wary of decoys. Like other dabbling ducks, mallards don't need a running start to become airborne; they spring up from the water into air.

(Dabblers are those that feed by dunking their heads below water while their tails tip up into the air, and by skimming the water surface with their bills. They rarely dive entirely underwater to feed.)

The seeds, leaves, and roots of water plants make up the bulk of a mallard's diet. Before lead shot was banned, the birds' dabbling habit meant that they often scooped up the spent shot with their food—and sometimes died of lead poisoning as a result.

The breeding female, and later her young, especially favor insects such as dragonfly nymphs, fly larvae, beetles, and grasshoppers. She usually lays eight to ten eggs in a well-hidden ground nest, most often near water. However, mallards have been known to nest at the base of trees or even in the notch of their branches, ten to twelve feet above the ground.

Shortly after the eggs are laid in the spring, the male usually abandons the family and gathers with other males. The drakes will molt, losing both their pretty colors and their ability to fly until their flight feathers regrow. After molting, the males look much like the females, but can be recognized by their yellow bills (the females' are orange with black markings). The drakes will molt once more before fall and then regain their breeding plumage.

Meanwhile, the female incubates the eggs for about a month, rarely leaving the nest. If a predator comes too close, she will fake a broken wing in an attempt to decoy it from the nest. Once the eggs have hatched, she waits only until her ducklings' down is dry before leading them into the pond or stream. The freshly hatched young immediately swim and dive, taking to it . . . well, like ducks to water.

By fall the brood will be able to fly. The mother will have molted, and will be ready to rejoin the males, who by this time are again wearing the breeding plumage that earns this bird its other common name of "greenhead."

They will be found on almost any freshwater pond, lake, stream, or flooded field, no matter how small, as long as there is aquatic vegetation to be eaten. These puddle ducks may be common, but given their long history of importance to people, mallards deserve a second look.

water shrew

Water and Marsh Shrews

Latin names: *Sorex bendirii* (marsh shrew); *S. palustris* (water shrew)

Description: Marsh shrew: 3½ inches long with 3-inch tail; dark fur, slightly lighter underneath. Water shrew: 3 inches long with 3-inch tail; dark fur with obviously lighter underside, including tail. Both species have short, stiff hairs on feet, small eyes and ears, and long, finely whiskered snouts.

Habitat: Marshes, streams, land bordering watery areas.

You're sitting on the bank of a small stream when an animal about the size of a mouse swims by underwater like a miniature submarine. The air trapped in its fur makes it appear coated with silver, and little bubbles string out in its wake. You've just seen a marsh shrew.

The Pacific Northwest boasts two shrews that are as comfortable in the water as they are on land. The marsh shrew (also called the Pacific water shrew) inhabits lower-elevation waterways, particularly marshes and streams, while the water shrew (or northern water shrew) prefers the same type of wet locations in upper elevations.

Both species have "swimming fringes" on the sides of their feet. These short, stiff hairs not only aid the animal in swimming, they also trap air so that, for a few seconds, the shrew can literally run across the water's surface. The fringe is most obvious on a young animal; it is apparently worn off in older ones and is not replaced. When a shrew submerges, its short, dense fur traps an insulating layer of air next to its body, and the shrew must paddle madly to counteract the air's buoyant effect. The moment it stops kicking, the shrew pops back to the surface.

But that silvery coating is crucial to the animal's ability to survive in the heat-robbing water. Because a shrew weighs so little compared to its body mass, it has a high rate of heat loss. To counteract this, the shrew's hyperactive metabolism demands a lot of calories, resulting in its notoriously voracious appetite. This small mammal is constantly a few hours away from starvation.

The marsh and water shrews' all-consuming drive to consume leads them to exploit both land and water food sources. In the water, a shrew can find aquatic insects, small fish, snails, leeches, and tadpoles as well as the eggs or larvae of various creatures. Terrestrial supplements include spiders, termites, earthworms, and slugs. The hunting shrew relies on its sense of touch and its acute hearing to track down its prey. A series of quick bites subdues the victim before it is consumed. Shrews usually haul aquatic prey to shore to be eaten, and excess food may be stored somewhere for a later meal.

Perhaps because of its demanding appetite, a shrew is loath to share its hunting area with others of its kind. Males and females must overcome their mutual hostility to encounter each other and mate—but they apparently manage to do so, since the females are either pregnant or taking care of young from February through August.

Shrews appear to be unpalatable to many would-be predators, but marsh and water shrews have at least one kind of aquatic and one kind of terrestrial enemy: trout and owls. Additional predators may include garter snakes, weasels, Pacific giant salamanders, and large frogs.

The marsh shrew, in particular, has not been well studied, even though both species are rather common in their respective habitats. They can be active any time of day but are most often out and about from dusk to dawn. With their adaptive ability to exploit both the water and the land as feeding territories, marsh and water shrews are like ravenous little amphibious assault vehicles.

Water

Whenever you add ice cubes to a glass of water, you're demonstrating why life can exist on planet Earth. Consider this: substances tend to contract and grow denser as they freeze. This is true of water, but only up to a point. At thirty-nine degrees F., water begins to act abnormally—it begins to expand and become lighter. As it freezes into a solid at thirty-two degrees F., it is lighter than it was when liquid. Thus, ice floats.

If ice were heavier than water, as natural law suggests it should be, it would sink. If it sank, the ice would lodge irretrievably on the beds of rivers, lakes, and freezing seas. The sun's rays, unable to reach the ice, would not be able to melt it. And as it sank, the ice would displace warmer water, causing it to rise to the surface, where it would freeze . . . and sink. Ice layers would build up until entire bodies of water were frozen solid, with only the thin upper sheet perhaps able to melt during the warmer months. In addition to making more of the world's water inaccessible to plants and animals, this process would drastically alter the world's climate. Bodies of water moderate Earth's temperatures by their ability to store the sun's heat and slowly release it. (A desert's wild temperature swings—below freezing at night and scorching during the day—are largely due to the absence of tempering water.) The daily temperatures of an icebound Earth would fluctuate over hundreds of degrees.

But raise your glasses high: ice floats! As a result, the fish and other creatures below the layer of ice in rivers, lakes, and seas survive by virtue of being insulated by that ice. And because ice is on the surface, it melts in response to the warming sun. In its melting, it reverts to gas and liquid; this trait is another of water's charms. Powered by the sun, water vapor rises from the oceans, is transformed to rain or snow in the upper atmosphere, and falls to earth in a never-ending cycle that recirculates, renews, and purifies water.

Except, perhaps, for input from incoming chunks of ice that vaporize as they strike Earth's upper atmosphere, the water we have today is the same supply the planet has always had. The hot water of your morning's shower might once have been part of a Neanderthal's streamside drink; the steam rising from your coffee may once have rained down upon a great auk or encased a woolly mammoth in ice.

Water is capable of many other feats. Over time, the "universal solvent" can disintegrate the strongest metal. Water's capillary action (the ability to climb against gravity) helps it to rise to more than four hundred feet in a Douglas-fir tree. Water is used to power steam engines and to generate electricity. It erodes rocks and entire canyons, straightens coastlines, levels mountains, floats boats and water striders, bursts pipes, and grows flowers—and every other living thing. All life requires water.

Everything alive is also composed of water to a greater or lesser extent, including people. Like Earth's surface, we humans are mostly water. Our water content averages sixty-five percent (a man's body is sixty-five to seventy-five percent water; a woman's water weight registers from fifty-five to sixty-five percent because of her greater amount of fatty tissue). Our brains are almost seventy-five percent water, our blood more than eighty percent—even our bones are almost twenty-five percent water. We require water to dissolve our food, carry nutrients and oxygen through our bodies, expel our waste, lubricate our eyes, joints, and soft tissues, and act as a coolant for our metabolic engines. For nine months we are carried in the amniotic fluid of our mother's womb; after our birth, water flows through us until the day we die.

Without water and all of its amazing properties, we humans, along with every other living thing—including Earth itself—would be left high and dry.

Selected References

Angell, Tony, and Kenneth C. Balcomb III. *Marine Birds and Mammals of Puget Sound*. Seattle and London: University of Washington Press, 1984.

Arnett, Ross H., Jr., and Richard L. Jacques, Jr. *Simon & Schuster's Guide to Insects*. New York: Simon & Schuster Inc., 1981.

Arno, Stephen F. *Northwest Trees*. Seattle: The Mountaineers, 1977.

Barker, Will. *Familiar Insects of America*. New York: Harper & Brothers, 1960.

Baron, Nancy, and John Acorn. *Birds of the Pacific Northwest Coast*. Renton, Washington: Lone Pine Publishing, 1997.

Behrens, David W. *Pacific Coast Nudibranchs: A Guide to the Opisthobranchs Alaska to Baja California*. Monterey, California: Sea Challengers, 1991.

Carefoot, Thomas. *Pacific Seashores: A Guide to Intertidal Ecology*. Seattle: University of Washington Press, 1983.

Coffey, D. J. *Dolphins, Whales, and Porpoises*. New York: Macmillan Publishing Co., Inc., 1978.

Corkran, Charlotte C., and Chris Thoms. *Amphibians of Oregon, Washington, and British Columbia: A Field Identification Guide*. Edmonton, Alberta: Lone Pine Publishing, 1996.

Davis, James Luther. *Seasonal Guide to the Natural Year: A Month by Month Guide to Natural Events*. Golden, Colorado: Fulcrum Publishing, 1996.

Ehrlich, Paul R., et al. *The Birder's Handbook: A Field Guide to the Natural History of North American Birds*. New York: Simon & Schuster Inc., 1988.

Evans, Howard Ensign. *Life on a Little-Known Planet*. New York: E.P. Dutton & Co. Inc., 1968.

Flaherty, Chuck. *Whales of the Northwest*. Seattle: Cherry Lane Press, 1990.

Flatow, Ira. *Rainbows, Curve Balls, and Other Wonders of the Natural World Explained*. New York: William Morrow and Company, Inc., 1988.

Ford, John K. B., et al. *Killer Whales*. Vancouver: University of British Columbia Press, 1994.

Gordon, David George. *Field Guide to the Geoduck*. Seattle: Sasquatch Books, 1996.

Guard, Jennifer B. *Wetland Plants of Oregon and Washington*. Redmond, Washington: Lone Pine Publishing, 1995.

Guberlet, Muriel Lewin. *Animals of the Seashore*. Portland, Oregon: Binfords & Mort, 1962.

_____. *Seaweeds at Ebb Tide*. Seattle: University of Washington Press, 1956.

Gunther, Erna. *Ethnobotany of Western Washington*. Seattle and London: University of Washington Press, 1973.

Haley, Delphine. *Seabirds of Eastern North Pacific and Arctic Waters*. Seattle: Pacific Search Press, 1984.

Harbo, Rick M. *Shells and Shellfish of the Pacific Northwest: A Field Guide*. Madeira Park, British Columbia: Harbour Publishing, 1997.

Harrington, H. D. *Western Edible Wild Plants*. Albuquerque: University of New Mexico Press, 1977.

Haskin, Leslie L. *Wild Flowers of the Pacific Coast*. Portland, Oregon: Binfords & Mort, 1967.

Hewlett, Stefani, and K., Gilbey Hewlett. *Sea Life of the Pacific Northwest*. Toronto, Ontario: McGraw-Hill Ryerson Lt., 1976.

Jacobson, Morris K. and David R. Franz. *Wonders of Jellyfish*. New York: Dodd, Mead & Co., 1978.

Kozloff, Eugene N. *Plants and Animals of the Pacific Northwest*. Seattle and London: University of Washington Press, 1978.

_____. *Seashore Life of the Northern Pacific Coast: An Illustrated Guide to Northern California, Oregon, Washington, and British Columbia*. Seattle: University of Washington Press, 1983.

Lamb, Andy, and Phil Edgell. *Coastal Fishes of the Pacfiic Northwest*. Madeira Park, British Columbia: Harbour Publishing, 1986.

Lawrence, Gale. *The Beginning Naturalist: Weekly Encounters with the Natural World*. Shelburne, Vermont: The New England Press, 1979.

Maser, Chris. *Mammals of the Pacific Northwest: From the Coast to the High Cascades*. Corvallis: Oregon State University Press, 1998.

Mathews, Daniel. *Cascade-Olympic Natural History: A Trailside Reference*. Portland, Oregon: Raven Editions, 1999.

Milne, Lorus, and Margery Milne. *National Audubon Society Field Guide to North American Insects and Spiders*. New York: Alfred A. Knopf, Inc., 1980.

Moss, Sanford, A. *Sharks: An Introduction for the Amateur Naturalist*. New Jersey: Prentice-Hall, Inc., 1994.

Niesen, Thomas M. *Beachcomber's Guide to Marine Life of the Pacific Northwest*. Houston, Texas: Gulf Publishing Company, 1997.

Peattie, Donald Culross. *A Natural History of Western Trees*. Cambridge, Massachusetts: The Riverside Press, 1953.

Ricketts, Edward F., et al. *Between Pacific Tides*. Stanford, California: Stanford University Press, 1997.

Schultz, Stewart T. *The Northwest Coast: A Natural History*. Portland, Oregon: Timber Press, 1990.

Steelquist, Robert. *Field Guide to the Pacific Salmon*. Seattle: Sasquatch Books, 1992.

Stokes, Donald W. *A Guide to Observing Insect Lives*. Boston: Little, Brown and Co., 1983.

Stokes, Donald W., and Lillian Q. Stokes. *A Guide to Animal Tracking and Behavior*. Boston: Little, Brown and Co., 1983.

_____. *A Guide to Bird Behavior, Volume III*. Boston: Little, Brown and Co., 1989.

Storm, Robert M., and William P. Leonard, eds. *Reptiles of Washington and Oregon*. Seattle: Seattle Audubon Society, 1995.

Swanson, Diane. *The Emerald Sea: Exploring the Underwater Wilderness of the Pacific Northwest and Alaska*. Anchorage: Alaska Northwest Books, 1993.

Terres, John K. *The Audubon Society Encyclopedia of North American Birds*. New York: Alfred A. Knopf, Inc., 1987.

Index